New Art for a New Era

New Art for a New Era

Malevich's Vision of the Russian Avant-Garde. From the
collection of the State Russian Museum, St Petersburg

Barbican Art Gallery
The State Russian Museum
Booth-Clibborn Editions

New Art for a New Era
Malevich's Vision of the Russian Avant-Garde
from the Collection of the State Russian Museum, St Petersburg
30 April – 27 June 1999
Barbican Art Gallery
Barbican Centre
London EC2Y 8DS

Exhibition organised at Barbican Art Gallery by:
Carol Brown and Philippa Alden
and at the State Russian Museum, St Petersburg, by:
Evgenia Petrova, Deputy Director, and Joseph Kiblitsky
Exhibition designed by Johnson Naylor

Barbican Art Gallery is owned, funded and managed by the Corporation
of London
Copyright © 1999 Corporation of London and State Russian Museum,
St Petersburg
Text and illustrations copyright © 1999 the State Russian Museum,
St Petersburg
Authors of the annotations and biographical details: Elena Basner, Irina
Boguslavskaya, Elena Ivanova, Olga Shikhireva, Natalia Solomatina,
Yulia Solonovich, Liudmila Vostretsova and Irina Zolatinkina

Catalogue edited by:
Evgenia Petrova, Deputy Director, State Russian Museum;
Mark Sutcliffe and Katharine Jacobson, Booth-Clibborn Editions;
Carol Brown and Philippa Alden, Barbican Art Gallery
Design: Robbie Mahoney
Translation: David Sheridan, Charlotte Hobson and Valentina Baslyk
Photography: Valery Kiuner and Vasily Vorontsov

First published in 1999 by Booth-Clibborn Editions
12 Percy Street, London W1P 9FB
in association with Barbican Art Gallery
and the State Russian Museum, St Petersburg

Distributed worldwide by Internos Books
12 Percy Street, London W1P 9FB
info@internos.co.uk
www.booth-clibborn-editions.co.uk

ISBN 1-86154-140-6

Printed in Hong Kong

Exhibition sponsored by:

Contents

Kazimir Malevich
57 Alogizm (Cow and Violin)
1913

After a number of years working with colleagues in the State Russian Museum, it gives us great satisfaction that *New Art for a New Era: Malevich's Vision of the Russian Avant-Garde* is being presented on the occasion of the Barbican Centre's *St Petersburg: Romance and Revolution* festival and accompanies the visits to our Centre of that city's other great institutions, the Kirov Opera, the St Petersburg Philharmonic Orchestra and the Maly Drama Theatre.

Three years ago, we received generous loans from the State Russian Museum for our *Diaghilev: Creator of the Ballets Russes* exhibition, including Bakst's splendid portrait of Diaghilev and his nanny. That lavish display revealed the gloss and excitement of the Tsarist era before aristocratic patronage dried up and the country fell apart at the seams with the Revolution in 1917.

Now, *New Art for a New Era: Malevich's Vision of the Russian Avant-Garde* provides a less flamboyant but more idealistic analysis of the subsequent period in the country's history when young artists were actively involved in the debates to define a cultural direction for the new Soviet state.

Revealing the mix of Malevich's genius for analysis, his cronyism as well as his antipathies, this exhibition is the first occasion that the State Russian Museum's painstaking study of its own collection's foundation has been shown to the Western world. It is a glowing example of the new Russian state's ability to explore its recent past without the anxiety of revealing unpalatable truths or stumbling against the objections of ideology.

This project has been guided from the start by Evgenia Petrova, the Deputy Director of the State Russian Museum, who with Vladimir Gusev, the Museum's Director, shares the credit for making this show happen. We join them in acknowledging the invaluable support of their colleagues: Irina Arskaya; Elena Basner; Irina Boguslavskaya; Elena Ivanova; Irina Karasik; Joseph Kiblitsky; Pavel Rosso; Olga Shikhireva; Natasha Solomatina; Yulia Solonovich and Liudmila Vostretsova.

From the British side, Jovan Nicholson has provided indispensable liaison and editorial work, while Her Majesty's Government and the Museums and Galleries Commission have allowed Barbican Art Gallery to benefit from the support of the Government Indemnity Scheme.

John Tusa Managing Director
John Hoole Art Galleries Director
Carol Brown Senior Exhibition Organiser

Introduction

By Dr V.A. Gusev, Director of the State Russian Museum

The State Russian Museum possesses the world's largest and most comprehensive collection of Russian avant-garde art. Although for fifty years, from the 1930s to the 1980s, severe ideological censorship meant that the collection was virtually unknown to the general public and even to the specialist, during recent years so many exhibitions have been mounted, and so much has been written and said on the subject, that it would seem difficult to avoid repeating the same themes for exhibitions and books based upon the same well-known names and 'set list' of works.

However, the richness of our collection has by no means been fully explored. As this exhibition confirms, there remains enormous potential for new discoveries and for revised interpretations of works that have suffered from stereotyped labelling or undeserved neglect.

The exhibition brings together a significant part of the collection that was assembled in the 1920s by the Petrograd Museum of Artistic Culture and subsequently transferred to the State Russian Museum. It is the first time this collection has been exhibited abroad in such a comprehensive and coherent way. The museum was a unique phenomenon in that many of the avant-garde's leading artists and ideologists, a group that included Kandinsky, Malevich, Tatlin, Punin, Matiushin, Filonov, and Mansurov, conceived and developed the collection themselves.

There can be few such instances of a group of artists belonging to roughly the same generation and – despite the diversity of their viewpoints and concepts – to a single movement successfully having created a conscious, collective expression of self-identification that has so radically changed the course not only of Russian art but of decorative art throughout the world in the twentieth century.

Today, with the benefit of a few decades' hindsight, it is possible to pinpoint certain weaknesses in the collection: some artists are represented by their less important works, some names are missing altogether, and the presence of others might seem fortuitous. Nevertheless, this look at the avant-garde 'from the inside', which is not simply an account by contemporaries and eye-witnesses but the self-expression of the participants and creators themselves, must give us more of the truth than subsequent interpretations. Indeed, this inside view proves surprisingly objective, refuting the perception of the avant-garde as isolated and exclusive. In fact the widest range of contemporary movements was included in these ideologists' field of vision, from the World of Art group to the Jack of Diamonds, from academic professionalism to intuitive primitive folk art, and so on.

It is important to remember when evaluating the collection assembled by the Museum of Artistic Culture over this short period that its activities were halted in mid-stream, its discussions effectively broken off in mid-sentence. In the summer of 1926 some 500 works – practically the entire collection – were transferred to the State Russian Museum. This was more than a simple change of legal ownership; it was a grim augury of the coming changes – in effect the beginning of the end of this brief but brilliant era of the Russian avant-garde.

This romantic and – alas – utopian idea of a fundamentally new institution was thus destroyed. The concept, born in the heat of revolution, was for a museum dedicated to enabling, in Malevich's definition, 'artist-scholars' not just to explore the patterns of artistic development but actively to create and display a new post-impressionist, post-revolutionary professional art culture. The idea collapsed and with it went the results of all the work, discussions, arguments and debates of those who had naively believed in the possibility of a romantic alliance between the proletarian revolution and art culture.

It is true that numerous documents and minutes relating to that time show that the transfer was undertaken perfectly voluntarily and that it was approved and authorised for a whole series of reasons. A commission had been set up as early as 1924 'for the establishment of links between the Art Department of the State Russian Museum and the Museum of Fine Art Culture'. Even some of the artists themselves – Tatlin and Mansurov, among others – repeatedly talked about the expediency of such a move.

The warning expressed as early as 1919 by Anatoly Lunacharsky, Commissar of the People's Commissariat for Enlightenment, proved prophetic: 'If we are to adhere exclusively to the point of view of pictorial culture, then it will be necessary to reorganise such museums every five years, for each group of artists will look upon this culture in a different way.' (*Art of the Commune*, No.11, 16 February 1919, p.3.)

For the sake of historical accuracy other, more worldly, reasons for the transfer to the State Russian Museum should also be mentioned. Over the course of its short existence the Museum of Artistic Culture slowly began to fall apart from the inside, partly because of constant differences in theoretical and creative ideas and partly as a result of personality clashes, individual ambitions, and struggles over the leadership, with relations between Tatlin and Malevich being particularly strained. In the end there were simply too many brilliant individuals involved for the group to work effectively as a team.

It is entirely natural that the founders of the Museum of Artistic Culture – this 'central focus in the fight against state museum management' – should themselves very quickly conclude that a union, and then a merger, with their principal antagonist – the State Russian Museum – was both unavoidable and essential.

Today it is clear that these artist-rebels' impulsive and at first sight occasionally inconsistent actions were dictated by an intuitive, almost subconscious, presentiment. They realised that in the end their ideological misdemeanours and liberties could not fail to antagonise the strengthening totalitarian regime and that the pressure being exerted on them was gradually hardening. It may have seemed that they were running counter to their own beliefs by burying their inspiration for ever within 'the sturdy tomb of art history', as Malevich called traditional state museums; in fact their action saved this wonderful collection from the repression that was to follow.

It is true that the collection languished in storerooms for several long decades, but at least it did not vanish altogether (as was the case, for example, with the collection of the similarly unrealised Museum of Artistic Culture in Vitebsk). Now at last its time has come.

To mark its centenary in March 1998, the Russian Museum opened an exhibition entitled *Museum within a Museum*, which included practically the entire collection of the Petrograd Museum of Artistic Culture. Moreover, the exhibition was set out in accordance with a scholarly reconstruction of the original idea, its structure determined by the avant-garde artists' own conception of the central movements and develop-ments in contemporary art.

For this exhibition in London we have specially selected the most significant works from the collection, which enable a proper understanding of the integrity and striking originality of this singularly important chapter in the history of the Russian avant-garde.

a. The Myatlev House on St. Isaac's Square where the Museum of Artistic Culture and subsequently the Institute of Artistic Culture were based from 1919 to 1926

b. c. The Department of New Tendencies at the State Russian Museum 1927

a.

b.

c.

Towards Non-Objective Art: the Collection of the Museum of Artistic Culture
By Evgenia Petrova

The collection of the Museum of Artistic Culture was assembled between the late 1910s and the first half of the 1920s. By then it was already clear that Russian art – for so long influenced by Europe – had produced its own leaders with defined movements that were distinctive from Cubism and Futurism.

The exhibition entitled *0.10* (late 1915/early 1916), also known as *The Last Futurist Exhibition of Paintings,* can be regarded as symbolic in that it presented a culmination of the various developments in Russian art of the early twentieth century. The exhibition gave emphasis to a crucial new direction in Russian art, namely Suprematism (from *supremus* meaning highest). Kazimir Malevich, Suprematism's leader and ideologist, defined *0.10* as an attempt by like-minded artists to take art beyond the limits of zero. Those who took part in the exhibition, including Malevich, Rozanova, Popova, Udaltsova, Klyun, Senkin and Morgunov, had already moved beyond Cubism and Futurism and starting from the point of zero had discovered a new direction for art.

1915 was the year in which Suprematism was intro- duced to the public. Artists had of course been working on Suprematist paintings for some time, and abstract art – similar in concept to Suprematism (though distinguished from it by Malevich) – had appeared in painting even earlier. As early as 1911 Vasily Kandinsky had published his pamphlet *On the Spiritual in Art*, in which he defined abstract art as one of the creative forms that most exactly expresses human emotion. His abstract paintings of the early 1910s vividly illustrated this theory.

At virtually the same time as Kandinsky, Mikhail Larionov offered his own interpretation of abstract art, creating a movement called Rayism, while Pavel Filonov and Mikhail Matiushin were also producing work and formulating theories based upon a dismantling of identifiable form.

Each of these leaders had his supporters and opponents, and together they made up a 'choir of many voices', united in their belief in what Malevich termed 'active art'. From the mid 1910s to the early 1920s this new way of looking at the world and of understanding art found its expression in numerous exhibitions.

Such was the sheer variety and importance of new artistic ideas being generated by artists eagerly engaged in the conceptual, theoretical side of art – of whom there was a considerable number in Russia at the time – that it became necessary to organise their work systematically. A series of museums and institutes was therefore created in Petrograd and Moscow, as well as in several provincial towns.

The most complete and effective of these new organisations proved to be the Museum of Artistic Culture in Petrograd. It succeeded in assembling a unique body of work (which later formed the basis for a research centre – Ginkhuk, the Institute of Artistic Culture), as well as other works intended to provide public instruction in the developments of twentieth- century art.

Despite all their arguments and differences of opinion, the museum's ideologists embraced a vision that was not simply limited to the very latest tendencies in art such as abstract art or Constructivism. Its organisers, which included Malevich, Vladimir Tatlin, Pavel Mansurov and Pavel Filonov, clearly had no intention of creating the museum in order to immortalise their own ambitions. The facts speak for themselves: the museum contained only seven paintings by Malevich, three by Tatlin (plus one of his counter-reliefs) and four by Filonov (with three of his drawings). Unfortunately the museum did not possess a single painting by Mansurov, who is now not so well known but who was a highly talented representative of the Russian avant-garde, playing an important role in art from 1910 to the 1920s.[1]

The aim of the museum's creators was to research and exhibit the developmental processes behind the plastic and painterly arts leading up to abstract art. They traced the beginnings of abstract art to the Impressionists and followed its development through Cézanne, Picasso, Van Gogh, and other Cubist and Futurist artists, all of whom had sought in various ways to deconstruct the outward appearance of form – an approach that remains the stylistic basis for twentieth- century art.

A significant part of the collection was devoted to the work of the Russian forerunners of such pioneers in abstract art as Kandinsky and Malevich. The museum's ideologists wanted to show characteristic features of a distinctly Russian direction in art and not simply the influences of Impressionism and Post-Impressionism.

Ilya Konchalovsky
Tray and Vegetables, 1910
Oil on canvas. 73 × 92 cm
Collection of the State Russian Museum

Natalia Goncharova
Hoar-Frost, 1910–11
Oil on canvas. 101×132 cm
Collection of the State Russian Museum

Ilya Mashkov, Piotr Konchalovsky, Aristarkh Lentulov, Alexander Kuprin and Robert Falk, who were all members of the Cézanne-influenced Jack of Diamonds group, were presented in the museum not just as followers of Cézanne but as artists inspired by their own folk art and city culture, and in particular by folk painting on wooden items such as trays and shop signs, and by *lubki* (popular prints). Thus, while Mashkov's *Still Life with Begonias* or Lentulov's *City* (p.29) are clearly influenced by Cézanne, Mashkov's *Boy in a Painted Shirt* (p.27) is much closer in its flamboyant plasticity and brightness of colour to folk art and in particular these types of painted wooden articles. Similarly, along with Goncharova's more Futurist works such as *Cyclist* (p.63) and *Factory* (p.62), the collection included such paintings as *Peasants* (p.41) and *Laundresses* (p.40), their inspiration deriving from Russian Primitivism, and *Winter* (p.39), which seems to share the graphic qualities of carved wooden bread-boards.

The organisers' attitude towards Goncharova's *Hoar-Frost* (p.11) and *Portrait of Larionov and his Platoon Commander* (p.38), and towards Larionov's *Acacias in Spring* (p.24), is instructive. These works were placed within a section entitled 'Impressionism and the movement towards Cézanne', with a comment referring to the clear influence of the Russian *lubok* – as in Larionov's *Venus* (p.37).[2] It would be wrong, however, to interpret such commentaries as an attempt by the museum's ideologists to find Russian roots in everything. Malevich, Tatlin, Filonov, Mansurov and Nikolai Punin cannot be accused of nationalism. When selecting works for the museum they carefully analysed the system within which each artist worked and these had to correspond to specific criteria within the development of art; they had to fit absolutely the concept and form of a particular movement. Thus Kandinsky's paintings, Malevich's Suprematist compositions and Rodchenko's works were all categorised within the so-called group of abstract or non-objective artists. Equally, some paintings were said to illustrate a transitional stage in art, something Malevich called the 'additional element'. Liubov Popova's *Portrait of a Philosopher* (p.67) is described in the following way: 'the meaning of the portrait has been almost totally transformed by the composition, which is only one step away from replacing a superficial identifiable appearance with abstraction.'[3]

The works were not exhibited according to artist but were distributed throughout various sections of the museum; the purpose was to give a comprehensive picture of the development of the latest tendencies in Russian art. Hence, Malevich's *Self-Portrait* (p.23) and *Still Life with Fruits* (p.22), both 1908, were shown in the section 'Impressionism and the movement towards Cézanne'; his *Portrait of I.V. Klyun* (p.61), 1913, was

placed in the Cubism section; and *Suprematism*, *Suprematism No. 58* and *Red Square* (p.109), all 1915, came within the section devoted to abstract art. As well as these recognised movements (Impressionism, 'Cézannism', Cubism, Futurism, Suprematism and Constructivism), Organic Culture, under Mikhail Matiushin, was also represented in the museum.

A section entitled 'Separate Individual Systems', which included paintings by Filonov, Kandinsky and Petrov-Vodkin, was also identified. It is true that Petrov-Vodkin was not concerned with issues that preoccupied the radical artists of the early twentieth century. His work developed along different lines and he became particularly interested in themes of social significance and daily life, and the use of space. He loved icons and the Italian Renaissance masters, and all these interests are apparent in his figurative canvases such as *Midday* (p.59) and *Violin* (p.56). Even though his more innovative contemporaries did not share Petrov-Vodkin's preoccupations, they nonetheless held his work in great respect and considered it worthy of inclusion in the Museum of Artistic Culture. In the cases of Kandinsky and Filonov it was a rather different matter. Today it is difficult to understand why the museum's ideologists excluded these artists from their study of the development of abstract art, placing them instead in the 'Individual Systems' section. Malevich's definition of abstract art and Suprematism as two separate movements was clearly influential. All the same, the Museum of Artistic Culture acquired five superb works by Kandinsky (four of which are included in the Barbican exhibition) and four wonderful paintings by Filonov (of which two are in the exhibition).

The organisers of the museum subscribed to a broad awareness of artistic culture and this is evident in the inclusion of works by artists of the World of Art movement, such as Alexander Benois, Mstislav Dobuzhinsky, Dmitry Mitrokhin and Sergei Chekhonin. Despite the fact that Benois, the movement's leader, was one of the harshest critics of the new tendencies, the World of Art group played a crucial role at the time and many of the innovative artists of the early twentieth century, such as Goncharova and Larionov, made their debuts at World of Art exhibitions. When they created the Museum of Artistic Culture, its ideologists considered it essential to include paintings by artists from the World of Art movement.

A number of less celebrated artists are also represented in the museum's collection – and rightly so for they played a significant role in the art world from 1915 to the 1920s. Alexei Grishchenko, Alexander Ivanov, Piotr Lvov, Alexei Morgunov, Sergei Senkin and Sofia Dymshits-Tolstaya are not well known today, but most of them exhibited alongside Malevich's Suprematist works at the *0.10* exhibition and all of them took part in

Vasily Kandinsky
Twilight, 1917
Oil on canvas. 91·5 × 69·5 cm
Collection of the State Russian Museum

Pavel Filonov
White Picture, 1919 (?)
Oil on canvas. 89 × 72 cm
Collection of the State Russian Museum

exhibitions over the period. Their inclusion is significant because it allows for a more complete understanding of the developments in avant-garde art than would have been possible had the museum limited itself only to famous names.

The works of art were generally selected on a proportional basis. The exceptions often had nothing to do with the personal predilections of individual members of the selection committee but, rather, were dictated by circumstance. Thus the museum's large holding of works by Olga Rozanova – some twenty canvases – is explained by her early death in 1918, which left everyone stunned and determined to keep a record of her artistic developments. These paintings follow Rozanova's progress from Fauvism or Neo-Primitivism (*Red House*, 1910 (p.30); *The Smithy*, 1912 (p.33); *In a Café*, 1912–13 (p.32) to Cubo-Futurism (*Writing-Desk*, 1916, p.73)) and finally to abstract art (*Non-Objective Compositions*, *c*.1915-16, pp.112–115).

A special section in the museum was devoted to works on paper, which were selected according to the same criteria as the paintings – for their artistic quality and adherence to a graphic system of development. Again the central aim was to show a progression leading to abstract art but, of course, with the graphic arts this was not so straightforward. Abstract artists preferred to work mainly on canvas, and thus it was harder to categorise the collection of drawings, watercolours and prints. The museum acquired a number of drawings and watercolours by Ivan Puni and Lev Bruni. Both artists convincingly convey in their work a feeling of the late 1910s and 1920s: Puni's is a world of city squares and hidden corners, shown through unexpected perspectives of colour compositions, with displacements and planes; Bruni, on the other hand, combines a more monochrome vision of daily life (*Mandelstam at his Desk*) with abstract compositions. Certain motifs found in these drawings clearly influenced the painting of the period – the laconic and precise artistic expression of themes that corresponded with the spirit of these revolutionary times and the circumstances under which the artists worked.

Vladimir Kozlinsky's linocuts are of a completely different style, but they too reflected the age and appealed to the museum's ideologists with their simplicity and clearly expressed revolutionary themes combined with a poster-like directness and purity of technique. Alexander Rodchenko and Varvara Stepanova, also richly represented in the museum's collection, vividly conveyed the ideas of Constructivism in their graphic works.

Russian icons were included in the museum's collection, as well as objects of folk and industrial art, posters and other polygraphic material. However, exact inventories of these departments have not survived, and the exhibits themselves were transferred when the museum was disbanded in the second half of the 1920s, to be distributed among various departments of the State Russian Museum as well as other museums in Russia.

By the time the Museum of Artistic Culture was transferred almost in its entirety to the State Russian Museum in the mid 1920s, it constituted a distinctive and comprehensive record of the new tendencies in Russian art of the first two decades of the twentieth century. As the works of art were chosen from exhibitions and studios directly by those participating in the process, the Museum of Artistic Culture acquired, almost without exception, the best and most important works that epitomise the avant-garde movement between 1900 and the 1920s. Naturally, works completed after 1926, such as Malevich's *Peasant Cycle* and his Suprematist Compositions from 1928 to 1932, were not part of the museum's collection, but it is true to say that its early avant-garde collection portrayed the entire spectrum of innovative Russian art of the period.

This exhibition devoted to the Museum of Artistic Culture is not the first time that Russian art has been shown at the Barbican Centre. We are all the more grateful, therefore, to our English colleagues and, especially, to John Hoole, Art Galleries Director and Carol Brown, exhibition curator, at the Barbican Centre, and to Jovan Nicholson of the British Council for his sincere interest in Russian art and for his excellent cooperation.

Notes
1. Pavel Mansurov left Russia to go to Italy on a business trip in 1928; from 1929 he lived in France and died there. Most of his works are located in France. For more on Mansurov see *Pavel Mansurov and the Petrograd Avant-Garde*, [ex. cat], St Petersburg, 1995 (also available in French).

2. See the section entitled 'Documents' in *Museum within a Museum: The Russian Avant-Garde from the Collection of the Museum of Artistic Culture in the State Russian Museum*, St Petersburg, 1998, p. 382 (I. Karasik).

3. Ibid, p.373.

Kazimir Malevich
Peasant Woman, 1928–32
Oil on canvas. 98·5 × 80 cm
Collection of the State Russian Museum

Kazimir Malevich
Suprematism, Female Figure, 1928–32
Oil on canvas, 196 × 126 cm
Collection of the State Russian Museum

The Petrograd Museum of Artistic Culture
By Irina Karasik

The concept of the Museum of Artistic Culture was inspired and implemented by some of the leading lights of the Russian avant-garde, notably Tatlin, Malevich, Kandinsky, Punin, Filonov and Rodchenko. Numerous other artists took part in the discussions and organisational work, including Shterenberg, Falk, Drevin, Udaltsova, Stepanova, Karev, Altman, Lapshin and Tyrsa.

The idea behind these new museums arose primarily from the age-old conflict between 'new art' and the traditional museum practice which ignored its very existence. 'New artists,' wrote Malevich, 'have been forced to spend their lives holed up in cellars and attics, be spat upon by the press and society, just so that future museum staff can reap the benefits of their valuable work.'[1] But now, carried along on the wave of revolution, artists declared themselves 'the only people who are properly able to address issues relating to contemporary art, for only those who are themselves the source of artistic merit should oversee the acquisition of contemporary art and be in charge of the country's artistic education'.[2] However, the purpose of the museum was not simply to correct this perceived injustice, which was only a cause, not a reason. Malevich once referred to the creation of the new museums as 'an important moment of organised artistic strength'.[3]

Indeed, for the new artists who were seeking to give their inventive and experimental work the status of a universal methodology, this was truly an act of social and creative self-determination. It was a logical step for an art that sought, through theories and manifestos, to analyse its own creative tools.

'We, as witnesses to and creators of the New Art movement,' affirmed Malevich, 'must also document it so that its history need not be dug out of the ruins of posterity with a combination of spadework and guesswork; so that the future museum worker or curator will have access to precise documentation.'[4]

The Museum of Artistic Culture can thus be seen, to some extent, as a self-portrait of the new art. As if sensing how short-lived their current ascendancy was likely to be, the artists undertook to organise their own 'memorial'. Rather than await the usual allotted time, they wanted to become part of history immediately, not at the whim of others but 'in their own image'. Later events, of course, showed this impatience to be fully justified. The Museum of Artistic Culture – the 'memorial to themselves' – which the innovators of the new art established, albeit temporarily, in their own lifetime, was for a period the only mark of freedom in a totalitarian regime.

The founders of the Museum of Artistic Culture had no interest in presenting art in the traditional way: as a succession of changes in individual styles and historical fashions or as a reflection of the age. Here, in place of the historian-cum-registrar stood the artist as creative designer. Artistic movements were studied and exhibited as logical and objective processes in the development of the professional plastic arts through their fundamental elements: material, colour, space, time/movement, form and technique; the 'moment of invention' and the 'moment of craftsmanship' were the key aspects.[5]

The creative processes involved in forming a work of art, its artistic methodology, became the central reason for exhibiting it in the museum; in other words, it was more a case of museum as laboratory than museum as art conservation or gallery.

The original intention was to broaden the scope of the new museum beyond purely contemporary material and to demonstrate how this artistic methodology could be applied to art of all ages and cultures. However, such a wide-ranging project that would have required a general redistribution of works from numerous museums was soon abandoned and only certain historical works of art were chosen: those which seemed to share some kindred, structural link with the new art, stemming identifiably from the same source or tradition, such as icons, Russian and Oriental prints, and other forms of folk art. Therefore, in 1922 the Petrograd Museum of Artistic Culture added 50 icons to its collection, at the same time requesting several duplicate fragments of Buddhist paintings from the ethnographic department of the Russian Museum. Similar pronouncements were made regarding the need for prints (lubki), painted signs and trays, all precipitated by a desire to trace 'the links between the new pictorial trends and Ancient Russian, Oriental and contemporary folk art.'[6]

Another idea considered was to combine within the collections of the Petrograd Museum of Artistic Culture and the Moscow Museum of Painterly Culture both Russian and Western-European art. This would have been achieved by redistributing the Shchukin and Morozov collections of French art in Moscow (artists specifically mentioned were Monet, Pissarro, Renoir, Sisley, Signac, Cézanne, Braque, Friesz, Matisse, Derain, Marquet, Picasso, Rousseau and Maillol), the rationale being that these works represented 'a starting point for examining contemporary trends in art and for analysing issues relating to painting'.[7] However nothing came of the idea.

The Museum of Artistic Culture was unquestionably aimed at the professional, and yet it was the founders' intention that this 'museum of the artist' could and should become as much a museum for visitors and schools, providing instruction not in art history but in 'reading the plastic arts'. It was precisely the technical and professional nature of the new museum that made it, in the eyes of its organisers, 'essential for the masses, since nowhere in the world up to now has a collection existed that can lead them to an appreciation of this aspect of painting, without which a true understanding of art is unthinkable'.[8]

The general concept of the Museum of Artistic Culture was proposed by the Fine Arts Department (IZO) of the People's Commissariat for Enlightenment (Narkompros) and approved at a museum conference in Petrograd in February 1919. Preliminary organisational work started at once and resulted in the creation of the Petrograd Museum of Artistic Culture and the Moscow Museum of Painterly Culture; corresponding collections in provincial towns were also planned.[9]

The Petrograd Museum of Artistic Culture can thus be regarded as the first of many art institutions created by the Russian avant-garde in the years immediately following the revolution. Works of art were chosen and displayed according to an ethos based upon a methodological zeal, a belief in an identifiable, objective logic in the development of art. These principles of applying analytical research to artistic creativity were also fundamental to the new methods of teaching, which resulted in the foundation of unique educational centres such as the Higher Artistic and Technical Workshops (Vkhutemas) in Moscow.[10] This belief in an objective analysis, the conviction that artistic work 'wants to measure and be measured',[11] led to the establishment of specific academic institutes where the artists themselves worked: the Institutes of Artistic Culture in Moscow[12] and Petrograd. 'For us the contemporary form in art is the research institute,' wrote Malevich.[13] It was not simply fortuitous that these institutions developed a close interrelationship: the Moscow Museum of Painterly Culture was affiliated to the Higher Artistic and Technical Workshops, which in turn was closely linked to the Institute of Artistic Culture in Moscow (Inkhuk); the same people were frequently involved with both institutions. As for the Petrograd

a. Nikolai Punin, Kazimir Malevich and Mikhail Matiushin at the Institute of Artistic Culture 1925

b. Kazimir Malevich at the Institute of Artistic Culture 1925

c. Pavel Filonov 1917

d. Alexander Rodchenko 1916

e. Mikhail Matiushin 1910

a.

b.

c.

d.

e.

Institute of Artistic Culture (Ginkhuk), it developed from the museum of the same name.

The history of the Petrograd Museum of Artistic Culture is linked primarily with the names of Punin, Altman, Tatlin, Malevich, Taran, Matiushin, Mansurov and Lapshin.[14] Of these, Punin played an unquestionably important role, second only to Malevich. They were both involved, to a greater extent than the others, in the conceptualisation of the new museum of contemporary art and in its practical realisation. Punin was largely responsible for defining the collecting ethos and general museum policy in the early stages, and Malevich, having assumed the leadership of the Museum of Artistic Culture in 1923, transformed it into a unique academic institute (the Petrograd Institute of Artistic Culture; 1924–26) – a legendary chapter in the history of the Russian avant-garde.

The teaching at the Institute of Artistic Culture focused upon the processes and laws governing the plastic arts, the specific ways and mechanisms in which contemporary systems of painting had evolved, and the methodology of an objective analysis of the spatial arts, with emphasis on the principles and procedures of natural and scientific knowledge. Malevich compared the institute to a bacteriological institute, 'which researches into various forms of bacteria and embryos, helping to explain behavioural changes in a given organism'.[15] The museum's exhibits were reformulated and presented within the institute as part of well-defined research installations. The Petrograd Museum of Artistic Culture was thus transformed under Malevich's leadership into a proper museum with a defined status for exhibits that were included according to strictly regulated criteria.

The museum first opened to the public on 3 April 1921 in the so-called Myatlev House on St Isaac's Square and included only paintings displayed 'according to the type of things – logically (not by artist)',[16] ranging from Impressionism to Dynamic Cubism. In 1922 a special 'evaluation commission', comprising Punin, Tatlin, Taran and Lapshin, developed the concept for a new layout, which was designed to show the 'central thread linking new Russian art'[17] – in other words artistic movements from Impressionism to Cézanne and through to Cubism, including Cubism's related movements. With their new display the artists also took into consideration 'the influence of folk art – primitive art, icons, and signs'.[18] The professional quality, or 'madeness' (sdelannost) of the object, was the criterion by which the actual works of art were chosen.

In January 1925, under Malevich's leadership, the exhibition area was redesigned (acquiring the layout regarded today as the definitive Museum of Artistic Culture). The museum's holdings at that time comprised 359 paintings, 18 sculptures and 186 drawings.[19] Its new layout was designed to present 'a full, visual exposition of [the institute's] research achievements',[20] by attempting to combine museum and 'laboratory' material in one general display area. It showed contemporary art as a logical process of development from one creative system to the next, starting with Impressionism, then 'Cézannism', through to Cubism (and its related movements), Futurism and Suprematism. Malevich explained the regular pattern by which each system changed into the next, calling his theory (no doubt influenced to some extent by Marxist terminology) 'the theory of the additional element'. He defined this as a kind of pictorial algorithm, with the structure and form of each system being characterised and completely reshaped by elements engendered within the framework of the previous system. Malevich expounded his theory by specifically identifying certain of these 'additional' elements: the fibrous curve of Cézanne, the crescent-shaped curve of Cubism, and the flat surfaces of Suprematism.

Free-standing exhibits exemplifying two further systems – Constructivism and 'organic culture' (the work of Matiushin and his pupils) – were added to the existing five-system display. Transitional and eclectic conditions were afforded special prominence, as was the presentation of individual pictorial viewpoints.[21]

The Museum of Artistic Culture mounted a number of exhibitions and was closely involved in educational work. In 1922 a retrospective exhibition took place entitled the Union of New Tendencies in Art, which included the work of many of those who by then were associated with the museum. 1923 saw the opening of an exhibition in memory of the Futurist poet Velimir Khlebnikov and, in the same year, Tatlin's workshop staged a performance of Khlebnikov's long poem Zangezi. From 1924 to 1926 several exhibitions of the research departments were organised.[22]

Evening lectures and debates on topical matters relating to art were also arranged. Among those who gave papers in 1922–3 were Malevich ('Light and Colour', 'New Evidence in Art'), Matiushin ('Space in the Work of the Artist'), Punin ('Content in the New Art'), Lapshin ('The Business of Painting') and Ermolaev ('The System of Cubism'). With its transformation into an institute, the bulk of the museum's work was taken over by the institute's Corporation of Academic Employees. Its members (including among others Ermolaev, Yudin and B. and M. Ender) established areas of responsibility within the museum and research departments; they helped visitors, gave lectures and took excursions.[23]

The creation of the research departments, and especially the museum's assimilation into the Petrograd Institute of Artistic Culture, meant that the status of the museum itself became less certain. The institute came under constant pressure to clarify whether the museum could continue to exist as part of the institute or whether its collection should be transferred to the State Russian Museum. Surviving information from high-level sources prove contradictory; many documents were found in the archives of the Petrograd Institute of Artistic Culture demanding a decision from the leadership as to the fate of the museum. In the institute itself opinion was split. Tatlin and Mansurov were all for handing the collection over to the Russian Museum, while Malevich, Matiushin and Punin considered it expedient to keep the museum as part of the institute.[24] However, in the spring and summer of 1926 the collections of the Petrograd Museum of Artistic Culture were finally transferred to the Russian Museum, where they formed the basis of the Department of the Latest Tendencies in Russian Art, headed by Nikolai Punin. The Museum of Artistic Culture's influence on this new department, in terms of its experience of collecting, exhibiting and research, is undeniable.[25]

Notes

1. Malevich, K. *The Museum of Artistic Culture*. Central State Archive for Literature and Art, St Petersburg, folio 244, op.1, d.18, p.30.

2. Declaration of the Fine Arts Department about the principles of museum management, resolved by the collegium of the department at a meeting of 7 February 1919. *Art of the Commune*, 16 February 1919.

3. Malevich, K. op. cit., p.30.

4. Ibid, p. 33.

5. See 'The Position of the Fine Arts Department of the People's Commissariat for Enlightenment concerning Art Culture', Art of the Commune, 16 February 1919: 'Moment of Invention' and 'Moment of Craftsmanship' – definitions of A. Rodchenko.

6. Central State Archive for Literature and Art, St Petersburg, folio 244, op.1, d.13, p.21 (reverse).

7. Ibid, d.6, p.17.

8. Short account of the Commission for organising the Museums of Painterly Culture. Russian State Archive for Literature and Art (Moscow), folio 665, op.1, d.7, p.1.

9. At the moment when the final decision was taken, 'many works of new art had already been collected; a fund for the Museum of Artistic Culture had already been formed'. (Malevich, K. *The Museum of Artistic Culture*, p.30). The Fine Arts Department of the People's Commissariat for Enlightenment had begun buying works by contemporary artists in 1918. The Moscow Museum of Painterly Culture (like the Petrograd museum) was founded in 1919. Its first director was Kandinsky. In October 1920 Rodchenko became head of the Moscow Museum of Painterly Culture, and in 1922 the directorship passed to P. Vilyams. In 1928 the Museum of Painterly Culture was put under the aegis of the Tretyakov Gallery and at the end of that year it was disbanded, its collection merging with that of the Tretyakov Gallery. See also: Dzhafarova, S. *The Museum of Painterly Culture*: The Great Utopia. ex. cat., Berne-Moscow, 1993.

10. The Higher Artistic and Technical Workshops (Vkhutemas) were set up in the autumn of 1920. They included an art faculty (painting and

Vladimir Tatlin 1920

Poster for *Zangezi* 9 and 11 May 1923

sculpture) and a production faculty (architecture, metalwork, textiles, woodwork etc.), which were combined in a general introductory course for all students based upon the formal-analytical methodology of the Russian avant-garde. The teachers included Kandinsky, Tatlin, Rodchenko, Popova, Vesnin and Korolev. In 1927 Vkhutemas was renamed Vkhutein (Higher Artistic and Technical Institute), and in 1930 it was disbanded.

11. Punin, N. 'The Measure of Art', *Art of the Commune*, 2 February 1919.

12. The Moscow Institute of Artistic Culture was founded in 1920 under the Fine Arts Department of the People's Commissariat for Enlightenment on the initiative of Kandinsky, Rodchenko and Babichev. Its activities were linked to the concept of Constructivism and a programme of industrial art.

13. See Rakitin, V., *Nikolai Suetin*, St Petersburg, 1998, p. 85.

14. The first director of the Petrograd Museum of Artistic Culture was Natan Altman but he was quickly replaced by Taran (1921–3). After the latter's departure to Kiev in the summer of 1923, Malevich became director of the museum and turned it into a research institute.

15. Central State Archive for Literature and Art, St Petersburg, folio 244, op.1. d.53, p.192 (reverse).

16. Central State Archive, St Petersburg, folio 2555, op.1. d. 647. p.101 (reverse).

17. Central State Archive for Literature and Art, St Petersburg, folio 244, op.1, d.19, p.2.

18. Ibid, d.6, p.61.

19. Paintings formed the largest and most interesting part of the collection and included the main works of the leading representatives of the Russian avant-garde (*Acacias in Spring* and *Venus* by Larionov; *Winter*, *Peasants*, *Laundresses* and *Cyclist* by Goncharova; *Alogizm*, *Builder* and *Red Square* by Malevich; *Restaurant* and two Cubist Compositions by Udaltsova; *Portrait of a Philosopher* and *Objects* by Popova; *Dairy-Maids*, *White Painting*, and *Flowers of a Universal Blossoming* by Filonov; *Mirror* and *Red Jew* by Chagall; *Musicians* by Shevchenko; *Violin*, *Still Life with Letters* by Puni; *Sailor* by Tatlin; *Red House*, *The Smithy*, *In a Café* and *Four Aces* by Rozanova; *Black Spot* and *Composition No. 218* by Kandinsky; *Portrait of a Boy in a Painted Shirt* and *Still Life: Mirror and Skull* by Mashkov; *Red and Yellow* and *Black on Black* by Rodchenko; *Man with a Horse* by Le Dantyu, and many others.

20. Central State Archive for Literature and Art, St Petersburg, folio 244, op.1, d.48, p.6.

21. Ibid, d.54, p.5.

22. Central State Archive, St Petersburg, folio 2555, op.1, d.805, p.38.

23. Lectures given included: 'The artist's conversion from the depiction of a likeness to the reworking of pictorial elements ('abstract composition')'; 'The concept of painting and its evolution in contemporary art'; 'The history of contemporary pictorial systems as a sign of the evolution in the perception of space'; 'The literary subject and pictorial contents of paintings'; 'Surface and volumetric-spatial consciousness'. (Central State Archive for Literature and Art, St Petersburg, folio 244, op.1, d.6, p.26).

24. Ibid, d.32, pp. 2 (reverse)-4 (reverse), 22-3; Central State Archive, St Petersburg, folio 2555, op.1, d.647, pp.88-90(reverse).

25. For further information see Karasik, I. 'The education and activities of the Department of the Latest Tendencies in Russian Art' in *History of the State Russian Museum*, St Petersburg, 1995.

Kazimir Malevich
63 Still Life (Fruits)
1908

Kazimir Malevich
62 Self Portrait
1908

Mikhail Larionov
50 Acacias in Spring
1904

Natalia Goncharova
26 Still Life with Fruits and an Open Book
1908–9

Ilya Mashkov
65 Winter City Landscape
*c.*1914

Aristarkh Lentulov
55 City
1910s (1917?)

Olga Rozanova
95 Red House
1910

Piotr Konchalovsky
41 Portrait of Yury Petrovich Denike (Yuriev) and
Anatoly Dmitrievich Pokrovsky (1890–1966)
1913

Olga Rozanova
97 In a Café
1912–13

Olga Rozanova
96 The Smithy
1912

Robert Falk
22 The Crimea: Lombardy Poplar
1915

Natalia Goncharova
29 Portrait of M.F. Larionov (1881–1964) and
his Platoon Commander
1911

Natalia Goncharova
27 Laundresses
1911

Natalia Goncharova
28 Peasants
(one of the nine-part composition Gathering Grapes)
1911

130 Sailor
1911

Iosif Shkolnik
105 Landscape
Early 1910s

Iosif Shkolnik
106 The Provinces
Early 1910s

Pavel Kuznetsov
49 Bird Market (Peacocks)
1913

Marc Chagall
13 Shop in Vitebsk
1914

Pavel Filonov
24 Flowers of a Universal Blooming
(from the series Towards a Universal Blooming)
1915

Vladimir Kozlinsky

42

43

44

46

Alexander Drevin
16 Refugee
1916

Boris Grigoriev
33 Land of the People
1917–18

Kuzma Petrov-Vodkin
69 Violin
1918

Kazimir Malevich
58 Portrait of I.V. Klyun (The Builder)
1913

Natalia Goncharova
31 Factory
1912

Natalia Goncharova
32 Cyclist
1913

Ivan Puni
73 Portrait of the Artist's Wife
1914

Liubov Popova   67
70 Objects   69
1915   126

Lev Bruni
4 Rainbow
1915

35 Plate on a Board
Late 1910s

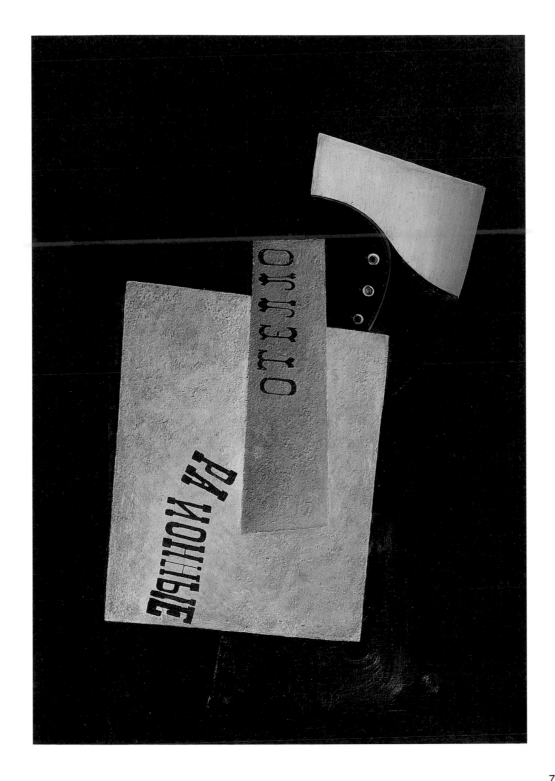

Vladimir Lebedev
54 Suprematism: Woman Ironing
Early 1920s

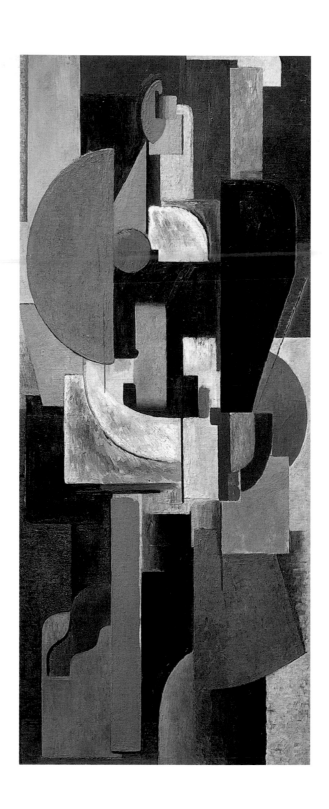

David Shterenberg

108 Sponge and Soap

1920

David Shterenberg
80

107 Still Life with Cherries
82

1919
130

Vasily Kandinsky
37 Black Spot
1912

Vasily Kandinsky
39 On White (Composition No. 224)
1920

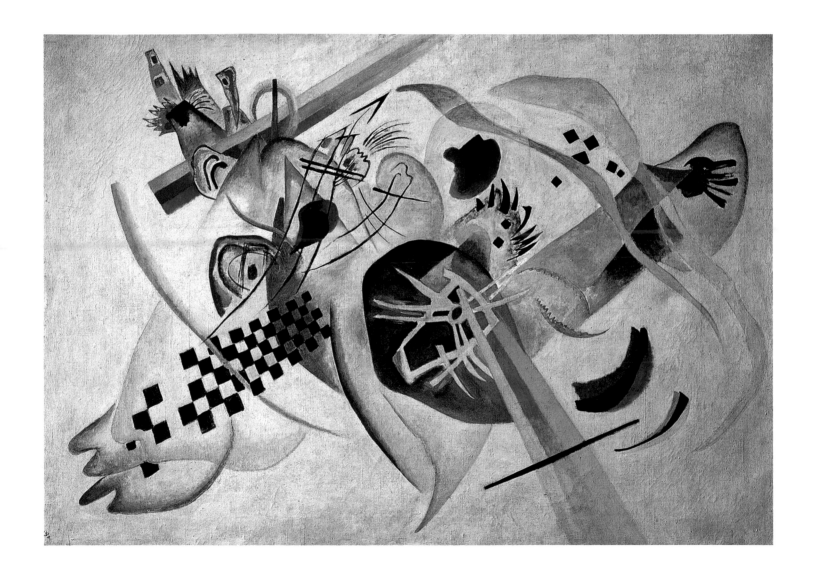

Ivan Puni
75 Violin
1919

Ivan Puni
74 Still Life with Letters, Spectrum Flight
1919

Alexander Rodchenko
76 Construction
1917

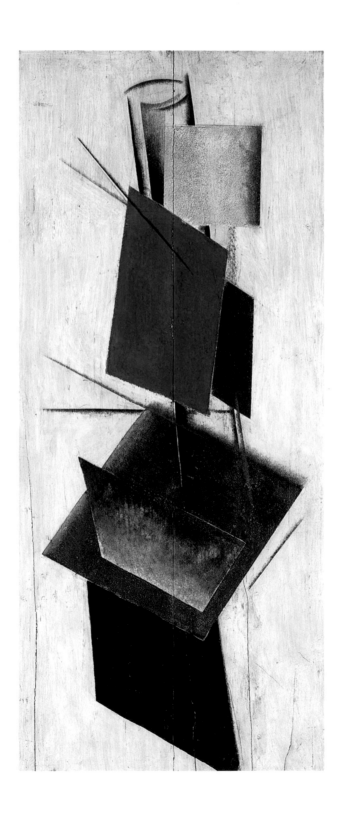

Alexander Rodchenko
79 White Circle
1918

Alexander Rodchenko
78 Black on Black
1918

Varvara Stepanova

112–127 From the series Figures

1919

112

113

114

115

116

120

121

122

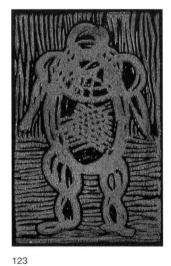

123

94

117

118

119

124

125

126

127

Sofia Dymshits-Tolstaya
18 Agit-Glass: Workers of the World, Unite!
1921[?]

98
99
119

Lev Bruni

6

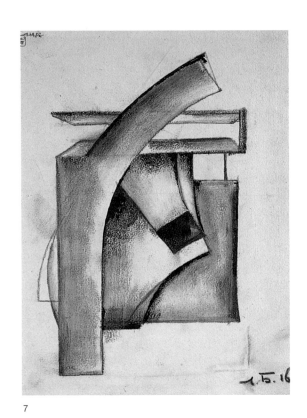

7

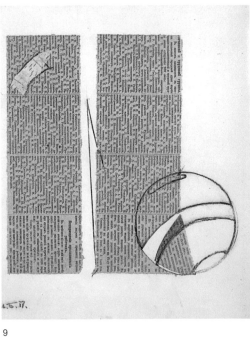

9

10

Sergei Senkin
103 Suprematist Composition
1922

106

Vladimir Stenberg
110 Colour Construction No. 4
1920

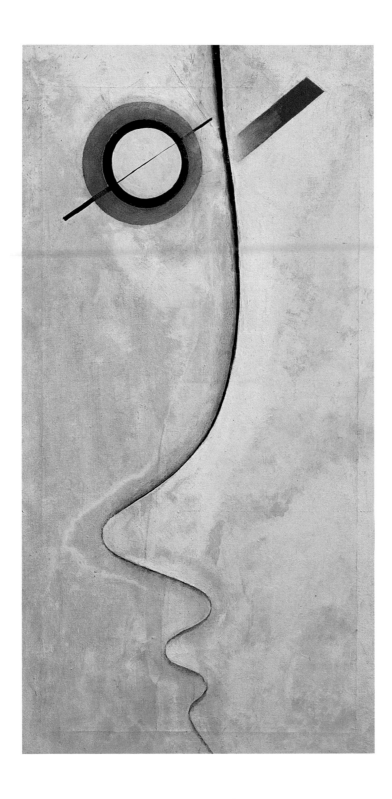

Kazimir Malevich
59 Red Square
1915

Kazimir Malevich
60 Suprematism
1915

Kazimir Malevich
61 Suprematism (Supremus No. 58. Yellow and Black)
1915–16

Olga Rozanova
99 Non-Objective Composition (Suprematism)
*c.*1916

Olga Rozanova
100 Non-Objective Composition (Suprematism)
c. 1916

Olga Rozanova
102 Non-Objective Composition (Suprematism)
c.1916

Olga Rozanova
101 Non-Objective Composition (Suprematism)
c.1916

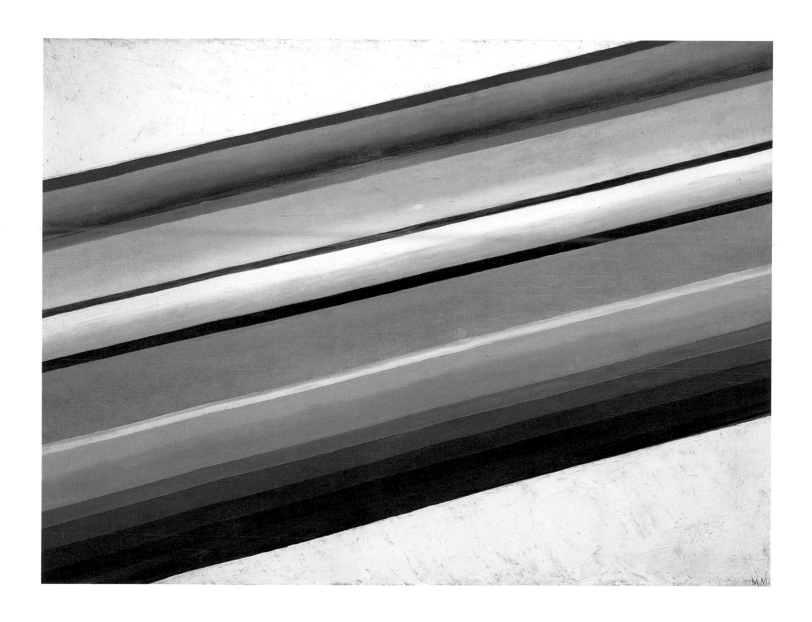

Natan Isaevich Altman
1889–1970

Painter, graphic artist, sculptor, stage designer and book illustrator. Studied at the Odessa School of Art (1901–7) under Kiriak Kostandi and G. Ladyzhensky, and at Maria Vasilieva's Free Russian Academy in Paris (1910–12). Took part in the following exhibitions: *Association of Southern Russian Artists* (1910); *World of Art* (1913, 1915–16); *Union of Youth* (1913–14); *The Last Futurist Exhibition of Paintings: 0.10* (1915); *Jack of Diamonds* (1916); and others. Member of the art associations L'Araignée (Paris, 1925), Young Europe (Paris, 1932), and the Association of Revolutionary Artists (Paris, 1934–5). Taught at the Petrograd State Free Art Studios (Svomas) (1918–20). Worked in the Fine Arts Department (IZO) of the People's Commissariat for Enlightenment (Narkompros) (1918–21). Lived in Paris (1929–35) and, from 1936, permanently in Leningrad.

Natan Altman was not one of the radical innovators of the time. His paintings are generally characterised by their allegiance to classical traditions and this sets him apart from artists more typically associated with the Russian avant-garde. Altman's traditionalism is particularly evident in his earlier works, from around the beginning of the 1910s, in which he employs the techniques of Cubism only as a means of emphasising the subject matter. In the words of the critic Abram Efros: 'Altman's portraits always show a likeness, his landscapes represent nature, and his still lives are true to the appearance of the original; but everything is so cunningly, tastefully, so cleverly and carefully seasoned with displacements, breaks, complexities of style, and multiple planes...'. At the same time, two works – *Still Life: Colour Volumes and Planes* (1918) and *Material Painting (Still Life with White Jug)* (1919) – are mature works of experimentation with form and execution and, in a broader sense, can be seen as an attempt to find a new way of organising space. [E.B.]

1 Self-Portrait, 1911 (p.74)
Tempera on paper. 46 × 33 cm
On the back of the paper: label of the Dobychina Gallery, Petrograd; pencil inscription: *23562*
ЖБ-1315

2 Still Life: Colour Volumes and Planes, 1918 (p.75)
Oil and gypsum on canvas. 59·5 × 43·5 cm
Signed and dated bottom right: *Нат. Альтман 18 г.* [Nat. Altman 18]; on the back of the canvas: label of the First State Free Art Exhibition, 1919; label of the Fine Arts Department (IZO) (torn); label of the Museum of Artistic Culture with the registration number *137/1926*
ЖБ-1570

3 Material Painting (Still Life with White Jug), 1919 (p.77)
Oil and enamel on canvas. 84·5 × 62 cm
Signed and dated bottom left: *Нат. Альтман 19 г.* [Nat. Altman 19]; on the back of the canvas: label of the Museum of Artistic Culture
ЖБ-1538

Lev Alexandrovich Bruni
1894–1948

Painter, graphic artist and monumentalist. Studied at Princess Tenisheva's School in St Petersburg (1904–9), at the Art School of the Academy of Arts (1909–12), and at Yan Tsionglinsky's studio in St Petersburg (1911), as well as the Académie Julian in Paris (1912). Participated in the following exhibitions: *World of Art* (1915); *Four Arts Society of Artists* (from 1925); *Makovets* (1920s). From 1920 to 1921 he taught at the State Free Art Studios (Svomas; formerly the Baron Stieglitz Central School of Technical Drawing) in Petrograd; from 1923 to 1930 at the Higher Artistic and Technical Studios, later the Higher Artistic and Technical Institute (Vkhutemas/Vkhutein) in Moscow; from 1930 to 1931 at the Moscow Textile Institute; and from 1931 to 1938 at the Moscow Institute of Decorative Art. From 1935 to 1948 he was director of the Studio of Monumental Painting at the USSR Academy of Architecture.

In their diversity of styles, Bruni's paintings included here are representative of the artist's experimentation over the first five years of his independent creative work. This was a period when Bruni assimilated the innovations of movements considered by his friend the art historian Nikolai Punin to be totally indispensable: Impressionism, Futurism and Cubism. At the same time it is surprising how easily and with what rare inconsistency Bruni manipulated these techniques. It is likely that his contemporaries valued him precisely for this talented inconsistency. Among Bruni's friends were Punin and the artists Miturich and Tyrsa. He was also greatly influenced in those years by such luminaries as Tatlin, Malevich, Rozanova, Puni, Klyun, Altman, Udaltsova and the poet Velimir Khlebnikov. *Rainbow* and *Segment of Mask* attest to the influence of Futurism and Suprematism, although in a fairly compromised way, as was recognised by Alexander Benois in his perceptive description of such experiments by Bruni as 'Academic Futurism'. The Russian Museum possesses two paintings by Bruni entitled *Rainbow*; this can be considered a preparatory study for the 1916 work. It is significant that the later painting was acquired by the Russian Museum in 1920 along with the first works to enter the art department's collection in Soviet times. In 1927 *Rainbow* was given special prominence in the display of the latest tendencies in art. The intricate abstraction of *Segment of Mask* clearly reveals, as does the later graphic series *Negatives,* Bruni's personal interpretation of Suprematism, a totality of plastic signs and symbols that are more comprehensible and accessible to the viewer's perception. [O.Sh.]

As a draughtsman, Bruni was singled out by Punin: 'The painter in him is inseparable from the draughtsman.' As with his painting, Bruni's drawings reflect various stages in his creative development. The most characteristic aspect of his early works is the expression of absolute form. Punin wrote: '...for Bruni form is the beginning and end of art; ...for form he is prepared to sacrifice beauty, skill, even composition and paint'. In this period Bruni was not depicting the world, but achieving an understanding of it. He was preoccupied by the play of successive forms that constantly arise, disappear, change; the idea of negative as positive; by the texture of the material: thick or transparent, glossy or rough. His compositions contain pieces of birch bark or scraps of paper with different surface qualities (such as tracing paper and newspaper). 'Building a composition, revealing forms, giving it a surface' – these were the central elements Punin noted in Bruni's drawings of this period. [L.V.]

4 Rainbow, 1915 (p.72)
Oil on canvas. 67 × 67 cm
Signed and dated bottom right: *Левъ Бруни 1915 годъ* [Lev Bruni 1915]
ЖБ-1512

5 Segment of Mask,* 1916 (p.103)
Oil on canvas. 82 × 57 cm
ЖБ-1620
* In documents of the Museum of Artistic Culture the title is given as *Segment*

6 Abstract Composition, 1916 (p.102)
Charcoal and tracing paper on paper. 37·1 × 20·9 cm
Initialled and dated in charcoal bottom right: *Л.Б. 16 г* [L.B. [19] 16]
On the back: graphite-pencil sketch of a multi-figured composition.
Р-34470

7 Abstract Composition, 1916 (p.102)
Charcoal, Indian ink, graphite pencil and chalk on paper. 28·2 × 22·3 cm; initialled and dated in charcoal bottom right: *Л.Б. 16 г* [L.B. [19]16]
Рб-7678

8 Circle and Glass Pipe, 1916
Charcoal on paper. 27·2 × 17·3 cm
Initialled and dated in charcoal bottom right: *Л.Б. 16 г* [L.B. [19]16]
Р-34469

9 Composition, 1917 (p.102)
Charcoal, newspaper and birch bark on paper. 34·5 × 31·5 cm
Initialled and dated in charcoal bottom left: *Л.Б. 17 г* [L.B. [19]17]
Рс-3044

Texts written by:

Paintings: Elena Basner [E.B.] Olga Shikhireva [O.Sh.] Drawings: Liudmila Vostretsova [L.V.] Irina Zolatinkina [I.Z.]

10 Negatives: Composition with a Cross, 1921 (p.102)
Ink on paper. 26·8 × 16·6 cm
Initialled and dated in ink bottom right: *ЛБ. 21* [LB. [19]21]
On the back: graphite-pencil sketch of puppy and ducklings; number of
the Museum of Artistic Culture in coloured pencil top right; *40,000* in
graphite pencil; *Негативы* [Negatives] in ink bottom left
Рс-3046

11 Negatives: Composition, 1921
Ink on paper. 26·4 × 16·7 cm
Initialled and dated in ink bottom right: *ЛБ. 21* [LB. [19]21]
On the back: graphite-pencil sketch of a bird; number of the Museum
of Artistic Culture in coloured pencil top right; *40,000* in graphite pencil
top left; *Негативы* [Negatives] in ink bottom left
Рс-3047

Marc Chagall (Mark Zakharovich Shagal)
1887–1985

Painter, graphic artist and monumentalist. Studied at the Yehuda Pen
School in Vitebsk (1906), the Drawing School of the Society for the
Encouragement of the Arts in St Petersburg (1907–8), Zaidenberg's
studio, the Zvantseva School of Drawing and Painting under Mstislav
Dobuzhinsky and Léon Bakst (1908–9), and in private studios in Paris
(1910–14). Took part in the following exhibitions: *World of Art* (1912);
Donkey's Tail (1912); *Salon des Indépendants* (Paris, 1912–14); *Jack of
Diamonds* (1916); and many others. From 1915 he lived in Vitebsk and
Petrograd and was director of the Vitebsk School of Art. In 1920 he
moved to Moscow where he worked in the Jewish Kamerny Theatre.
From 1922 he lived abroad, first in Berlin, then in Paris, and during the
war in the USA.

These paintings by Chagall date to his return from Paris, when he was
living in Vitebsk and then in Petrograd. Creatively they represent a new
stage in his work, returning to the motifs of his early childhood and
youth (*Shop in Vitebsk* and *Father*). These early war years were marked
by dramatic experiences in Chagall's creative life, and this is reflected in
full measure in such paintings as *Mirror* and *Red Jew*. *Red Jew*, one of
the most tragic pictures in the series devoted to the fate of the Russian
Jews, is a work of truly epic power. [E.B.]

12 Father, 1914 (p.47)
Tempera on paper mounted on cardboard. 49·4 × 36·8 cm
Signed and inscribed bottom right: *Chagall Отец 914* [Chagall, *Father*,
[1]914]; on the back of the cardboard in red: *1521 52*; label of the
Dobychina Gallery, Petrograd; label of the First State Free Art
Exhibition, 1919, with *No. 1521*; label of the Museum of Artistic Culture
ЖБ-1898

13 Shop in Vitebsk, 1914 (p.46)
Tempera on paper mounted on cardboard. 49 × 48·5 cm
Signed bottom right: *Шагалъ* [Chagall]; inscribed and signed by the
artist on the back of the cardboard: *Лавка в Витебскъ 1914 г.* [*Shop
in Vitebsk*, 1914, Chagall]; label of the Museum of Artistic Culture
ЖБ-1518

14 Mirror, 1915 (p.48)
Oil on cardboard. 100 × 81 cm
Signed bottom right: *Шагалъ* [Chagall]; inscribed on the back: *Отдел
И.И.* [Department of Fine Arts]; label of the Dobychina Gallery,
Petrograd, with a price of 500 roubles; label of the First State Free Art
Exhibition, 1919, with *No. 1536*; label of the Museum of Artistic Culture
ЖБ-1707

15 Red Jew, 1915 (p.49)
Oil on cardboard. 100 × 80·5 cm
Signed bottom right: *Chagall*; signed on the back of the cardboard:
Chagall 915; inscription of the Fine Arts Department; label of the First
State Free Art Exhibition, 1919, with *No. 1537*; label of the Museum
of Artistic Culture
ЖБ-1708

Alexander Davidovich Drevin
1889–1938

Painter and graphic artist. Studied at the Riga School of Art (1908–13)
under Vilgelm-Karl Purvit. Started to exhibit in 1911. Member and
exhibitor of the following associations: *Green Flower* (Riga, 1913);
World of Art (Petrograd, 1922); *Association of Extreme Innovators in
Painting* (Moscow, 1922); *Moscow Painters* (1925); *Association of Artists
of Revolutionary Russia* (1926); *Society of Moscow Artists* (1928); the
Thirteen group (1931). Worked in the Fine Arts Department of the
People's Commissariat for Enlightenment (Narkompros) (1918–20).
Taught at the Higher Artistic and Technical Workshops, later Institute
(Vkhutemas/Vkhutein) in Moscow (1920–30).

Drevin's *Refugee* is a typical example of Neo-Primitivism in Russian
painting of the mid 1910s, and reflects the strong influence of folk art,
in this case peasant wooden sculpture from the Baltic. The emotional
intensity, depth and seriousness of the work (which was painted during
the First World War) and its lack of irony, distinguishes it from other
works of the Neo-Primitives. [E.B.]

16 Refugee, 1916 (p.53)
Oil on canvas. 100 × 89 cm
Signed and dated on the back of the canvas: *Alexander Drewin 16*;
label of the Museum of Artistic Culture with *МХК 332 **1920* (*Девушка
в синем*) [Girl in Blue]
ЖБ-1404

Sofia Isaakovna Dymshits-Tolstaya [Pesatti]
1889–1963

Painter. Studied in St Petersburg under Sergei Egornov (1906–7) and at
the Zvantseva School of Drawing and Painting under Léon Bakst and
Mstislav Dobuzhinsky; then in Paris at the Académie de La Palette
under Charles Guérin (1910–11). Took part in the following exhibitions
from 1912: *World of Art*; *Jack of Diamonds*; *The Store* (1916); *Union of
New Tendencies in Art* (1922). From 1918, she was active in the organisation of the Fine Arts Department (IZO) of the People's Commissariat
for Enlightenment (Narkompros) and its All-Russian Exhibition
Committee; in the 1920s she was head of the commissariat's art
publications department and director of the painting section of the
Union of Art Workers in Leningrad. From the 1930s she worked much in
the genre of portraits and still lives, creating works corresponding to the
generally accepted norms of Socialist Realism, and from 1925 to 1935
she edited the art sections of the journals *Rabotnitsa* ['Working
Woman'] and *Krestyanka* ['Peasant Woman'].

These paintings by Dymshits-Tolstaya are characteristic of an
interesting period in the artist's creative life, when she was
experimenting with painting materials, inspired above all by the works
of Tatlin, whom she had met in the mid 1910s and who became a close
friend. Despite such associations, Dymshits-Tolstaya followed her own
course within the avant-garde movement. In her memoirs she wrote: 'I
was strongly influenced by Tatlin's counter-reliefs, but I myself couldn't
break away from flat surfaces. I found a wonderful material to experiment with – glass: although flat, it also had three-dimensional qualities
when worked from both sides'. In the years immediately following the
October Revolution, Dymshits-Tolstaya remained interested in painting
on glass, and it was not surprising that she was offered a glass-painting
studio in the reorganised Stroganov School in Moscow. However, she
had to turn this down because of her move to Petrograd with Tatlin in
1919. These years were marked creatively, as Punin wrote, by her far-
reaching 'research into painting materials', prime examples of which are
the works created from non-traditional materials, including the series of
works executed on glass. In 1922, at the *Union of New Tendencies in
Art* exhibition at the Museum of Artistic Culture, Dymshits-Tolstaya
showed five works dated 1921 under the general title *Agit-Glass*.
[O.Sh.]

17 Circus, before 1921 (p.99)
Oil, sand and bitumen on canvas. 112 × 75·5 cm
Inscribed in black paint on the back of the canvas: *Музейное бюро*

ИЗО 63 17 x 25 1/2 [Museum office of the Fine Arts Department
63 17 × 25 1/2]
ЖБ–1410

18 Agit-Glass: 'Workers of the World, Unite!', 1921[?] (p.97)
Oil on glass. 53·2 × 40cm
ЖБ–1590

19 Glass Relief, before 1921[?] (p.98)
Oil on glass. 39 × 44·2cm
ЖБ–1591

Alexandra Alexandrovna Exter
1882–1949

Painter, graphic artist and stage designer. Graduated from art school in Kiev (1906), studied in Paris at the Académie de la Grande Chaumière (1908). Between 1909 and 1914 she lived alternately in Kiev, Moscow and Paris and made a trip around Italy. Participated in the following exhibitions: *Link* (Kiev, 1908); *Wreath of Stefanos* (1909); *Jack of Diamonds* (1910–16); *Union of Youth* (1910 and 1913–14); *Tramway V: the First Futurist Exhibition of Paintings* (1915); *The Store* (1916); *5 x 5 = 25* (1921); *Exposition des Arts Décoratifs* (Paris, 1925); and others. Taught in her own studio in Kiev (1918–20) and at the Higher Artistic and Technical Workshops (Vkhutemas) in Moscow (1921–2). At the beginning of the 1920s she joined the Constructivists. Designed for the Moscow Art Theatre and the Kamerny Theatre, illustrated books, designed clothes, and worked in the cinema. From 1924 she lived and worked in Paris, teaching at Fernand Léger's Academy of Contemporary Art and in her own studio.

Exter's works dating to the mid 1910s reflect her decision to become allied to the Constructivists. If in the earlier, rather decorative *Still Life with Eggs* a movement away from realistic representation, through a Cubo-Futurist approach, is only hinted at, the composition dated 1917–18 represents a complete plastic construction in which, in the words of the critic Yankov Tugendkhold, 'only pure ideas of painting exist: the idea of space and depth, the idea of balance and movement'. [E.B.]

20 Still Life with Eggs, 1914 (p.70)
Oil on canvas. 88 × 70cm
On the back of the canvas: label inscribed *Александра Экстер Мертвая натура кв. № 744* [Alexandra Exter, *Still Life,* receipt No. 744]; label of the Museum Office of the Fine Arts Department (IZO); label of the Museum of Artistic Culture
ЖБ–1411

21 Non-Objective Composition, 1917–18 (p.96)
Oil on canvas. 88 × 70cm
On the back: label of the Museum Office of the Fine Arts Department (IZO); label of the Museum of Artistic Culture
ЖБ–1433

Robert Rafailovich Falk
1886–1958

Painter, graphic artist and stage designer. Studied at the Konstantin Yuon School of Drawing and Painting and at Ilya Mashkov's studio in Moscow (1903–4), then at the Moscow School of Painting, Sculpture and Architecture (1905–10) under Valentin Serov and Konstantin Korovin. Travelled to Italy (1910–11). One of the founders of the Jack of Diamonds group. Member and exhibitor of the following associations: *Jack of Diamonds* (1910-27); *World of Art* (1911–17, 1921–22); *Moscow Painters* (1925); *Association of Artists of Revolutionary Russia* (1925–8); *Society of Moscow Artists* (1925–8). Lived and worked in Paris (1928–37), then in Moscow.

Falk's work represents a special phenomenon even within the Jack of Diamonds group to which he belonged: he and Kuprin are usually known as the 'quiet Jacks'. From the very beginning Falk's painting was distinguished by its lyricism, psychological profundity, and a subtlety of artistic perception, which was not entirely characteristic of the Jack of

Diamonds artists. His relationship to the avant-garde movement should be mentioned only with the greatest care. At the same time, one sees in Falk's work a reflection of the more general artistic laws by which Russian painting developed in the 1910s, with his keen interest in questions of colour and form, inherited first and foremost from Cézanne. [E.B.]

22 The Crimea: Lombardy Poplar, 1915 (p.34)
Oil on canvas. 108 × 88cm
On the back of the canvas: label of the Museum of Artistic Culture
ЖБ–1426

23 Portrait of an Unknown Man [undated] (p.35)
Oil on canvas. 137 × 114cm
On the back of the canvas: label of the Museum of Artistic Culture
ЖБ–1505

Pavel Nikolaevich Filonov
1882 (1883 new calendar)–1941

Painter, graphic artist, stage designer and poet. Studied at the Painting and Decorating Workshops in St Petersburg (1897–1901) and at the L.E. Dmitriev-Kavkazsky School of Painting and Drawing (1903–8) whilst simultaneously attending drawing classes at the Society for the Encouragement of the Arts, and at the art school of the Imperial Academy of Arts (1908–1910). In 1907 he made a trip to Palestine (via Constantinople); from 1911 to 1912 he travelled to France and Italy and in 1905 along the Volga and to the Caucasus. From 1910 he participated in exhibitions. In 1910 he was one of the founder members of the Union of Youth group. Exhibited as a member of the following associations: *Non-Party Society of Artists* (1913); *Union of Youth* (1910–14); *Community of Artists* (1921–2). In 1914 he organised a workshop for painters and draughtsmen of *Sdelannye Kartiny* ('Made Paintings') and published a manifesto, the second edition of which was completed in 1923 ('Declaration of Universal Flowering'). In 1913 he was co-designer with Iosif Shkolnik for Mayakovsky's tragedy *Vladimir Mayakovsky*. Between 1914 and 1915 he wrote the poetic work *Propoven o prorosli mirovoy* ('The chant of universal flowering'). From 1923 he served in the department of general ideology at the Museum of Artistic Culture and worked on the statutes for the State Institute of Artistic Culture. In 1925 he established the Masters of Analytic Art group from students at the Higher Artistic and Technical Institute (Vkhutein), which existed unofficially up to 1941.

The works of Filonov, a distinctly individual artist, were highly valued by his contemporaries. *German War* is a characteristic example of the artist's work before the Revolution. Filonov's idea of a universal flowering led him to seek in his painting a way of showing the concept of a lost harmony in human existence. In their subject matter many of Filonov's pictures are influenced – though not necessarily overtly – by the artist's anti-urban tendencies. Filonov believed the city to be a terrible, destructive weapon of all that is spiritual. *German War*, painted during the war years, is closer in style to the Cubo-Futurist works of Malevich, Klyun and Popova. It is painted in a subdued palette of grey-brown. The artist's desire to capture the dynamics and chaos of destruction is paramount; shapes are splintered into fragments only to reunite in a new form. [O.Sh.]

24 Flowers of a Universal Blooming, 1915 (p.50)
(from the series *Towards a Universal Blooming*)
Oil on canvas. 154·5 × 117cm
ЖБ–990

25 The German War, 1915 (p.51)
Oil on canvas. 176 × 156·3cm
ЖБ–987

Natalia Sergeevna Goncharova
1881–1962

Painter, graphic artist, stage designer and book illustrator. Studied sculpture at the Moscow School of Painting, Sculpture and Architecture (1901–9). Painted independently, visiting the studio of Konstantin

Korovin and profiting from the advice of Mikhail Larionov, with whom she became one of the initiators of the first *Jack of Diamonds* exhibition (1910) and exhibitions of the *Donkey's Tail* (1912), *Target* (1913) and *No.4: Futurists, Rayists, Primitives* (1914). She also participated in the following exhibitions: *Golden Fleece* (1908–10); *Union of Youth* (1910–12); *Post-Impressionists* (London, 1912); *Der Blaue Reiter* (Munich, 1912); and the First German Autumn Salon (Berlin, 1913). Author and illustrator of Futurist books and a leading designer for Diaghilev's theatrical productions, on whose invitation she left for Switzerland in 1915, together with Larionov, and thence to Italy. From 1919 she lived permanently in Paris.

Goncharova was one of the leaders of the early Russian avant-garde, an artist who followed a complicated path from 'impressionistic' studies to the first attempts in the history of Russian painting at abstract art. However, the high point of her creative work is justly ascribed to the period of Neo-Primitivism when Goncharova's interest in sources drawn from folk art was enriched by her fine knowledge of the latest western art. This period lasted until the end of the 1900s to early 1910s. Its culmination came in 1911 with such masterpieces as *Laundresses*, *Winter*, *Hoar-Frost*, and, of course, the grandiose nine-part series *Gathering Grapes*, one part of which is the painting *Peasants*. Her slightly later works such as *Factory* and, especially, *Cyclist*, reflect Goncharova's subsequent enthusiasm for Futurism. In *Factory* she employs only certain Futurist techniques, in particular linear and plane displacements. As for *Cyclist*, this work can be considered to be one of the most characteristic examples of Futurist painting, not only in Goncharova's work but in Russian art of the early 1910s as a whole. [E.B.]

26 Still Life with Fruits and an Open Book, 1908–9 (p.25)
Oil on canvas. 112 × 121 cm
Inscribed by the artist on the back of the canvas: *Вне каталога № с ц. 800 p* [ex catalogue No. c price 800 roubles]; label of the Museum of Artistic Culture
ЖБ-1594

27 Laundresses, 1911 (p.40)
Oil on canvas. 102 × 146 cm
Inscribed by the artist on the back of the canvas: *№ 560 ц. 600 p* [price 600 roubles]; label of the Museum of Artistic Culture
ЖБ-1321

28 Peasants (one of the nine-part composition *Gathering Grapes*), 1911 (p.41)
Oil on canvas, 131 × 100·5 cm
Inscribed by the artist on the back of the canvas: *№ 564 ж ц.об 6000 p* [price 6,000 roubles]; label of the Museum of Artistic Culture
ЖБ-1592

29 Portrait of M. F. Larionov (1881–1964) and his Platoon Commander, 1911 (p.38)
Oil on canvas. 119 × 97 cm
Inscribed by the artist on the back of the canvas: *№ 572 ц. 500 p.; Н.С. Гончарова Портретъ М.Ф. Ларіонова и его взводнаго Москва Тверская Трехпрудный пер. свой д. № 1/2* [No. 572 price 500 roubles; N. S. Goncharova *Portrait of M. F. Larionov and his Platoon Commander* Moscow Tverskaya Trekhprudny Lane House 1/2]; label of the Museum of Artistic Culture
ЖБ-1593

30 Winter, 1911 (p.39)
Oil on canvas. 118 × 99 cm
On the back of the canvas: label of the Museum of Artistic Culture
ЖБ-1599

31 Factory, 1912 (p.62)
Oil on canvas. 102·5 × 80 cm
Artist's monogram and inscription on the back of the canvas: *НГ № 610 ц. 500 p.* [NG No. 610. Price 500 roubles]; label of the Museum of Artistic Culture
ЖБ-1601

32 Cyclist, 1913 (p.63)
Oil on canvas. 78 × 105 cm
On the back of the canvas: label of the Fine Arts Department (IZO) with *No. 2897*; label of the Museum of Artistic Culture
ЖБ-1600

Boris Dmitrievich Grigoriev
1886–1939

Painter and draughtsman. Studied at the Stroganov Central Art School (1903–7) under D. Shcherbinsky, and at the Academy of Arts in St Petersburg (1907–12) under A. Kiselev and N. Dubovsky. Took part in the following exhibitions: *Impressionists* (1909); *Salon des Indépendants* (1912–13); *World of Art* (1913, and 1915–18; from 1918 he was also a member of the group). Lived in St Petersburg, then from 1919 in Finland, Germany and France.

Land of the People or, as Grigoriev himself called it in his list of works, *Land of the Peasants*, is organically linked with the artist's *Raseya* cycle of pictures completed at the same time. Contemporaries wrote of the artist's ability 'to find in all the transience and illusiveness of life something deeper and more eternal…to create images of real art, cruel and truthful, as life itself' (N. Punin). This is clearly felt in *Land of the People*, in which Grigoriev, without idealising the Russian countryside or trying to simplify his complicated feelings towards it, manages to evoke that passionate 'love-hate' relationship to his homeland that has been described by numerous poets and writers during those years. [E.B.]

33 Land of the People, 1917–18 (pp.54–55)
Oil on canvas. 90 × 215 cm
ЖБ-989

Karl Voldemarovich Ioganson
c.1890–1929

Sculptor. In the 1910s he studied at the Riga City Art School and at the Penza School of Art (1915–16). After the October Revolution he served in the Red Latvian Gunners Regiment. A member of the Institute of Artistic Culture (Inkhuk) from 1920, where he was an active member of the Working Group of Constructivists (from 1921) and also a member of the production department. He participated in the discussion: 'Analysis of Concepts of Construction and Composition' (1921). He showed his spatial constructions at the Second Spring Exhibition of the Society of Young Artists (Obmokhu) (1921), and participated in the First Russian Art Exhibition at the Van Diemen Gallery in Berlin (1922).

Ioganson's *Abstract Drawing* dates to 1920–1 when Constructivism was in its formative stages. At the Institute of Artistic Culture in Moscow a Working Group of Objective Analysis was set up that included such well-known artists as Rodchenko, Stepanova, Popova, Medunetsky, Georgy Stenberg, Ioganson and others. The artists set out to discover the laws of form creation, to pinpoint the primary elements which make up constructions and to show how they are combined and revealed in the objective world. For Ioganson the primary element was the cross which he used as a basis for his compositions on paper and in his spatial constructions. Lines intersecting crossways determine the planes and forms, creating a powerful tension and organising the construction as a unified whole. [L.V.]

34 Abstract Drawing, 1920–1 (p.104)
Graphite, colour pencil and Indian ink on cardboard. 31·5 × 24 cm
Signed bottom right in Indian ink: *Иог…Ж-II* [Iog…Zh-II]
Inscribed in ink on the back: *Иогансон* [Ioganson]; below, a stamp of the Museum Office of the Fine Arts Department of the People's Commissariat for Enlightenment, 1921, No. 2644, Moscow; in coloured pencil in the centre: *521 (МХК)*
Ср6-21

Alexander Ivanovich Ivanov
1888–1948

Painter, monumentalist and graphic artist. Studied at the Zvantseva School of Drawing and Painting in St Petersburg (1908–11) under Kuzma Petrov-Vodkin. Took part in the painting of the cathedral in Kronstadt (1912–13). Participated in exhibitions from 1918, including *Moscow Painters* (1925), *Association of Artists of Revolutionary Russia* (1926) and the *Society of Moscow Artists* (1928–31).

Ivanov's name will mean little to today's visitor but some of his surviving works show that he is undeservedly neglected. In his paintings dating to the 1910s, Ivanov displays an interest in his classical heritage – in icon painting (evident in his use of straight and reverse perspectives) – and in Cubism and pictorial folk art. His works are distinguished by their sense of harmony and taste. [O.Sh.]

35 Plate on a Board, late 1910s (p.76)
Oil on canvas. 72 × 60·5 cm
ЖБ-1449

Vasily Vasilievich Kandinsky
1866–1944

Painter, graphic artist and art theorist. Studied at the Faculty of Law at Moscow University (1885–93). He received his artistic education at the art school of Anton Ažbe (1896–7) and then at the Academy of Franz von Stück (1900) in Munich. One of the founders of the Phalanx exhibiting society (1901). Organiser of the Neue Künstlervereinigung München (Munich New Artists Association) (1909). Took part in the following exhibitions: Salon of Vladimir Izdebsky (1909–11); *Jack of Diamonds (*1910, 1912); *Salon des Indépendants* (Paris, 1905, 1908); *Der Blaue Reiter* (Munich, 1911–12; together with Franz Marc published the almanac of the same name); *Der Sturm* (Berlin, 1913). Member of the artists' collegium of the Fine Arts Department (IZO) of the People's Commissariat for Enlightenment (Narkompros) (1918); head of the Moscow Museum of Painterly Culture (1919–20). From 1921 he lived in Germany, and from 1933 in France.

Kandinsky's work occupies a unique position in the art of the Russian avant-garde, not only because he lived and worked for many years in Germany (both before and after the Revolution) with the result that his artistic creativity belongs in equal measure to the Russian and German cultures. In the 1910s, when the majority of Russian painters were striving to achieve a higher, 'impersonal' essence in art – a new artistic canon that surpassed the creative individuality of the artist – Kandinsky took a path that led ever deeper into the subconscious, attainable only through intuition. The four works from the Russian Museum's collection trace the main stages in Kandinsky's creative development: *St George*, a variation of a well-known motif, does not break entirely with his figurative beginnings, while *Black Spot* is already an example of his mature abstract painting. Towards the end of the 1910s and the beginning of the 1920s, the central internal quality of these works – an emotional tension – gradually gives way to a pure dispassionate abstraction (*On White*). [E.B.]

36 St George (2nd variation), 1911 (p.84)
Oil on canvas. 107 × 95 cm
Signed, dated and inscribed by the artist on the back of the canvas: *Кандинскій – Георгій 1911* [Kandinsky – George 1911]; label of the Museum of Artistic Culture; label on the stretcher: *L.O. & S.95.78*
ЖБ-1698

37 Black Spot, 1912 (p.85)
Oil on canvas. 100 × 130 cm
Signed and dated bottom left: *Kandinsky 1912*; inscribed on the back of the canvas: *No. 99 22 1/2 x 29 1/4*; label of the Museum of Artistic Culture; inscribed on the stretcher: *Кандинскій № 30* [Kandinsky No. 30]
ЖБ-1323

38 Two Ovals (Composition No. 218), 1919 (p.86)
Oil on canvas. 107 × 89·5 cm
Artist's monogram and date bottom left; inscribed and dated by the artist on the back of the canvas: *No. 218 1919;* label of the Museum of Artistic Culture
ЖБ-1406

39 On White (Composition No. 224), 1920 (p.87)
Oil on Canvas. 95 × 138 cm
Artist's monogram and date bottom left; artist's monogram, inscription and date on the back; label of the Museum of Artistic Culture
ЖБ-1610

Ivan Vasilievich Klyun (Klyunkov)
1873–1942

Painter and draughtsman. Initial artistic education in Warsaw and Kiev (1890s); at the beginning of the 1910s he visited the studios of Feodor Rerberg and Ilya Mashkov in Moscow. Took part in the following exhibitions: *Moscow Salon* (1911, 1914); *Union of Youth* (1913–14); *Tramway V: the First Futurist Exhibition of Paintings* (1915); *The Last Futurist Exhibition of Paintings: 0.10* (1915); *The Store* (1916); *Jack of Diamonds* (1916); and others. Member of the Stankovists Society (from 1925) and the Four Arts Society of Artists (1925–7). Lived and died in Moscow.

Klyun was a devoted follower of Malevich, whose acquaintance he made in 1907. He passed through similar stages to Malevich in his creative life, beginning with his distinctive variations of Symbolism and art nouveau, and culminating in Suprematism, before finally returning to figurative painting at the end of the 1920s. *Gramophone* belongs to Klyun's Cubo-Futurist period and bears all the distinctive traits of that movement, combining the spatial dimensions of Cubism with the plastic dynamics of Futurism. [E.B.]

40 Gramophone, 1914 (p.71)
Oil on canvas. 80·5 × 76 cm
Signed and dated top left: *Клюн 1914* [Klyun 1914]
On the back of the canvas: label of the Museum Fund with *No. 353*; label of the Fine Arts Department (IZO) with *No. 625*; label of the Museum of Artistic Culture
ЖБ-1690

Piotr Petrovich Konchalovsky
1876–1956

Painter. Studied at the school of drawing in Kharkov, at evening classes of the Stroganov Central Art School in Moscow, at the Académie Julian in Paris (1897–8) and then at the Higher Art School of the Academy of Arts in St Petersburg (1898–1905). Visited the workshop of Konstantin Korovin at the Moscow School of Painting, Sculpture and Architecture (up to 1909). Travelled in France, Italy and Spain (1904–13). One of the organisers of the first *Jack of Diamonds* exhibition (1910), and participated in all its subsequent exhibitions (1912–27). Took part in the following exhibitions: *Salon d'Automne* (Paris 1908, 1910); *Salon des Indépendants* (Paris, 1910–12); *Golden Fleece* (1910); *Moscow Association of Artists* (1911); and others. Founder-member of the society of Moscow Painters (1924–5).

Konchalovsky's mature paintings represent the influence of 'Cézannism' in Russian art, a movement that was central to the work of artists who exhibited at the first *Jack of Diamonds* exhibition in 1910. However, this influence was combined in Konchalovsky's work with an interest in urban and folk art. One critic remarked of Konchalovsky's portraits that they contained 'as much of the shop sign and the popular print [*lubok*] as they do Cézanne's archetypes'. Within the avant-garde movement as a whole, Konchalovsky's work is characterised by its moderation, in common with other members of the Jack of Diamonds group, gravitating increasingly towards representation and the traditional tenets of painting. [E.B.]

41 Portrait of Yury Petrovich Denike (Yuriev) and Anatoly Dmitrievich Pokrovsky (1890–1966), 1913 (p.31)
Oil on canvas. 160 × 132 cm
Signed and dated top right: *П. Кончаловскій 1913* [P. Konchalovsky 1913]; on the back of the canvas: label of the exhibition of the Jack of Diamonds group with the inscription: *Портрет г. Д и г. П* [Portrait of Mr D. and Mr P.]
ЖБ-1902

Vladimir Ivanovich Kozlinsky
1891–1967

Graphic artist and stage designer. From 1907 he studied at the school of the Society for the Encouragement of the Arts, the Zvantseva School of Drawing and Painting under Léon Bakst and Mstislav Dobuzhinsky, and at the studios of D. Kardovsky, L. Shervud and M. Bernstein. From 1911 to 1917 he studied under V. Mate at the Art School of the Academy of Arts in St Petersburg. Took part in the following exhibitions: *Triangle* (1909); *Impressionists* (1909–10, Vilno); *Contemporary Painting* (1912, Ekaterinodar); *Russian Landscape* (1918, Petrograd). From 1918 he was a member of the Union of Youth. He participated in the First Free Art Exhibition (1919), the First Exhibition of Soviet Art (Berlin, 1922), and the Art Exhibition Celebrating the Tenth Anniversary of the October Revolution (1928). From 1918 to 1921 he taught at the etching workshop of the State Free Art Studios (Svomas). He decorated streets and squares in Petrograd for the first anniversary of the October Revolution and May Day celebrations. From 1920 to 1921 he was one of the organisers and head of the art department of the Russian Telegraphic Agency's Northern Region Office (the Petrograd ROSTA windows: revolutionary posters that used the forms of *lubok* folk prints for propaganda effect). In the 1930s he illustrated and designed books for the publishing houses *Sovetsky pisatel* [Soviet Writer] and *Academia*. Until the mid 1930s he lived in Leningrad before moving to Moscow.

In 1919 Kozlinsky worked on an album of etchings entitled *Contemporary St Petersburg* consisting of ten illustrations and a title page. The album, however, was not published. The artist simplified form and developed monumental plastic 'formulae' for depicting revolutionary heroes: a sailor, a worker and an agitator. The depiction of the sailor was understood by contemporaries as an attempt to create a new revolutionary *lubok* [popular print]. Kozlinsky's etchings demonstrated the connection between contemporary art and the traditions of folk art, in particular the *lubok*. The laconic and expressive language used in these lino cuts was subsequently repeated for the ROSTA windows. Nine lino cuts from the album were exhibited at the First Exhibition of Soviet Art in Berlin. [L.V.]

42 1st May, 1919 (p.52)
Graphite pencil, gouache and whitening on paper. 36·3 × 23·8 cm
Graphite-pencil inscription on the back, top right, with number of the Museum of Artistic Culture
Pc-605

43 Demonstration on the Embankment, 1919 (p.52)
Linocut. 34·5 × 20·4 cm
Graphite-pencil inscription on the back: *ОНТЕЧ* [ONTECH]; *No.8 /не приобр/для/МХК* [No.8 not acquired for the Museum of Artistic Culture]
Crp-1931

44 Meeting, 1919 (p.52)
Linocut. 29·5 × 21 cm
Engraved initials bottom right: *WK*; graphite-pencil inscription on the back: *Не приобретено/для МХК* [not acquired for the Museum of Artistic Culture]
Crp-1933

45 Sailor, 1919
Linocut. 33·1 × 22·1 cm
Etched initials bottom right: *B.K.* [V.K.]; graphite-pencil inscription on the back: *Не приобретено/для МХК* [not acquired for the Museum of Artistic Culture]
Crp-1935

46 The Street, 1919 (p.52)
Linocut. 31·7 × 21·6 cm
Crp-7327

47 Two Heads (Syphilitic and Prostitute), 1919
Linocut. 31·9 × 20·4 cm
Etched initials bottom right: *BK* [VK]
Crp-1991

Nikolai Ivanovich Kulbin
1868–1917

Artist and dilettante. One of the most active propagandists for the new art, initiator of art debates and exhibitions, author of articles and manifestos. *Privatdozent* of the Military Commercial Academy, doctor at General Headquarters with rank of acting Councillor of State. Received no professional artistic education. Organiser of the first exhibition of the avant-garde: *Contemporary Tendencies in Art* (1908). Founded the group Triangle (1910). Took part in the following exhibitions: *Impressionists* (1909); Salon of Vladimir Izdebsky (1909); *Jack of Diamonds* (1912); *International Futurist Exhibition* (Rome, 1914). Initiator of Marinetti's trip to Russia.

Nikolai Kulbin was instrumental in bringing together the various artistic currents of the Russian avant-garde. His own painting developed along Symbolist (for example *Artist*) and Neo-Impressionist lines. This apparent contradiction between his radical approach to the aims and ambitions of the new art and his own more moderated painting is something he shared with David Burlyuk and can be seen as a typological feature of the early Russian avant-garde. [E.B.]

48 Portrait of the Artist, 1916 (p.42)
Oil on nickel. 25 × 17·8 cm
Signed and dated bottom right: *Н. Кульбинъ 1916* [N. Kulbin 1916]
Inscribed, signed and dated by the artist on the back of the canvas: *Н. Кульбинъ "Художник" 1916 г. ц 75 р.* [N. Kulbin *Artist* 1916 price 75 roubles]; label of the Museum of Artistic Culture
ЖБ-1169

Pavel Varfolomeevich Kuznetsov
1878–1968

Painter, graphic artist, monumentalist and stage designer. Studied at the studio of the Saratov Society of Fine Art Lovers (1891–6), the Moscow School of Painting, Sculpture and Architecture (1897–1904), and in Paris at the studio of Filippo Colarossi and at other art studios. One of the organisers of the exhibitions *Alaya roza* ('Crimson Rose'; Saratov, 1904) and *Golubaya roza* ('Blue Rose'; 1907). Participated in the following exhibitions: *World of Art* (1911, 1912); *Golden Fleece* (1908, 1909). Chairman of the Four Arts Society of Artists (1924–31).

49 Bird Market (Peacocks), 1913 (p.45)
Oil on canvas. 76 × 92 cm
Signed bottom right: *П.К.* [P.K.]
ЖБ-1175

Although Kuznetsov took part in the work of the committee set up to organise the Museum of Artistic Culture, his involvement was short-lived, and it would be wrong to regard him as an artist of the Russian avant-garde. His work, which is more in the Symbolist tradition, shows that his interests lay elsewhere, and the two paintings by Kuznetsov in the Museum of Artistic Culture patently took second place to work that illustrated the main currents in the new Russian art. [E.B.]

Mikhail Feodorovich Larionov
1881–1964

Painter, graphic artist, stage designer and book illustrator. Studied at the Moscow School of Painting, Sculpture and Architecture (1898–1910, intermittently). Together with Serge Diaghilev took part in the organisation of the Russian section of the Salon d'Automne in Paris

(1906). Initiator of the first *Jack of Diamonds* exhibition (1910), and the exhibitions *Donkey's Tail* (1912), *Target* (1913), and *No.4: Futurists, Rayists, Primitives* (1914). Took part in the following exhibitions: *Union of Russian Artists* (1906); *Golden Fleece* (1908–10); *Union of Youth* (1910–12); *Der Blaue Reiter* (Munich, 1912); First German Autumn Salon (Berlin, 1913); and many others. Author of the first Futurist publications. Founder of Rayism – one of the first movements in abstract art (1912). Leading designer for theatrical productions of Diaghilev, on whose insistence he moved to Switzerland with Goncharova in 1915, and thence to Italy. From 1919 he lived permanently in Paris.

The two paintings by Larionov exemplify different stages in his creative work. *Acacias in Spring*, a classic example of Russian Impressionism (or, to be more precise, Neo-Impressionism) of the mid 1900s, is one of Larionov's masterpieces, reflecting the most profound, most lyrical side of his talent. It is imbued with a unique sense of internal harmony and spirituality. *Venus* represents Larionov's period of mature Primitivism. [E.B.]

50 Acacias in Spring, 1904 (p.24)
Oil on canvas. 118 × 130 cm
Signed on the back of the canvas: *Ларионов № 2* [Larionov No. 2]; label of the exhibition of the Union of Russian Artists; label of the Dobychina Gallery, Petrograd, with *No. 1028*; label of the Museum of Artistic Culture
ЖБ-1201

51 Venus, 1912 (p.37)
Oil on canvas. 68 × 85·5 cm
Inscribed by the artist: *Венера 1912 г. Михаил* [Venus 1912 Mikhail]
On the back of the canvas: label of the Museum of Artistic Culture
ЖБ-1528

Vladimir Vasilievich Lebedev
1891–1967

Painter, graphic artist and poster artist. Studied at F. A. Rubo's studio (1910–11); from 1910 was an occasional student at the Art School of the Academy of Arts in St Petersburg; from 1912 to 1916 he attended the M. D. Bernstein and L. V. Shervud School of Painting, Drawing and Sculpture in St Petersburg. Participated at exhibitions from 1909. From 1918 to 1921 he taught at the State Free Art Studios (Svomas; formerly the Baron Stieglitz School). In the 1910s he collaborated with *Satirikon*, *Argus* and other journals. From 1920 to 1922 he worked in the poster department of the Russian Telegraphic Agency's Northern Region Office (the Petrograd ROSTA Windows: revolutionary posters that used the forms of *lubok* folk prints for propaganda effect). He was the art editor of Detgiz Publishing House in Leningrad (1924–33).

Still Life with a Palette and *Still Life with a Boot* bear witness to Lebedev's interest in the achievements of two of the leading artists of his time: Tatlin and Malevich. If the former inspired Lebedev's experiments with the texture of the painting surface and work with non-traditional materials, then it is to Malevich that Lebedev is indebted for acquiring the expressive language of plastic formulae. *Suprematism: Woman Ironing* marked a new stage in the artist's creativity: his assimilation of Cubism, which still predominated in Russia as the point of departure for many artistic innovations. In its plastic resolution, clearly influenced by Cubism while at the same time demonstrating in the title a kinship with Suprematism, the work can be seen to some extent as an attempt to interpret nature and the roots of Suprematism. The ease with which Lebedev does this, unconstrained by artistic canons, makes this creative improvisation extremely expressive. On a number of occasions Lebedev emphasised the experimental nature of his Cubist compositions, such as *Woman Ironing*, by calling them *Cubism No.1*, *Cubism No.2* etc. He worked on his *Laundresses (Women Ironing)* series of paintings and drawings from 1920 to 1925. The series completed his Cubist experiments. [O.Sh.]

52 Still Life with a Palette, 1919 (p.78)
Oil on canvas. 89 × 65 cm
Signed and dated top left: *ВЛебедев 1919* [V. Lebedev 1919]
Label on the back of the canvas
ЖБ-1435

53 Still Life with a Boot, 1920 (p.79)
Oil on canvas. 107 × 77 cm
Signed and dated bottom right (partially missing): *ВЛеб/…/1920* [VLeb/…/1920]; label on the back of the canvas; label on the stretcher (partially missing)
ЖБ-1424

54 Suprematism: Woman Ironing, early 1920s (p.81)
Oil on canvas. 187 × 82 cm
Ж-10398

Aristarkh Vasilievich Lentulov
1882–1943

Painter and stage designer. Studied at the Penza School of Art (1889–1900, 1905), the Kiev School of Art (1900–05), and the studio of Dmitry Kardovsky in St Petersburg (1906–7); worked independently in Paris at Henri Le Fauconnier's studio (1911). Took part in exhibitions from 1907. Member of the following associations in which he also exhibited: *Jack of Diamonds* (from 1910); *Association of Artists of Revolutionary Russia* (1926–27); *Society of Moscow Artists* (1928–9). Also took part in the following exhibitions: *The Wreath* (1907); *Link* (1908); *The Wreath of Stefanos* (1908); *Union of Russian Artists* (1910); and *World of Art* (1911, 1912). From 1919 he headed the stage design workshops at the First Free Art Studios, and from 1920 the Stage Design Department of the Faculty of Painting at the Higher Artistic and Technical Workshops (Vkhutemas). From 1932 he taught at the Department for Promoting Qualifications for Theatre Artists at the Institute of Fine Art's Faculty of Painting in Moscow.

The landscapes *City* and *Monastery*, dating to the central period of Lentulov's creative work, reveal, in their brightness and energy of colour, the true talent of this most original painter in the Jack of Diamonds group. *City* is notable for the risks the artist takes with colour combinations and for its pulsating style. Using the techniques of Cubism, Lentulov virtually embraces abstraction. The artist's subsequent interest in Russian popular prints (*lubki*), which assumed greater significance in his work than Cubism, is clearly shown in *Monastery*, one of a series of views of the New Jerusalem Monastery outside Moscow. Lentulov's inherently festive, exalted perception of the world around him is given form through resonant colours and the rapid whirlpool of fragmented forms which break up and come together in a fantastical crystal. [O.Sh.]

55 City, 1910s (1917?) (p.29)
Oil on canvas. 86 × 69·5 cm
ЖБ-1430

56 Monastery, early 1910s (1917?) (p.28)
Oil on cardboard. 101·5 × 98 cm
Signed bottom left: *Лентулов* [Lentulov]; inscribed in red ink on the back: *Н. іерус. Витебск* [New Jerusalem. Vitebsk]; label of the Museum Fund with *No. 337*
ЖБ-1706

Kazimir Severinovich Malevich
1878–1935

Painter, graphic artist and art theorist. Studied at the Kiev School of Art (1895–6), and at Feodor Rerberg's studio in Moscow (1905–10). Took part in the following exhibitions: *Association of Moscow Artists* (1909–11); *Jack of Diamonds* (1910, 1916); *Donkey's Tail* (1912); *Target* (1913); *Union of Youth* (1912–14); *Salon des Indépendants* (Paris, 1914); *Tramway V: the First Futurist Exhibition of Paintings* (1915); *The Last Futurist Exhibition of Paintings: 0.10* (1915–16); and others. Collegium member of the Fine Arts Department (IZO) of the People's Commissariat for Enlightenment (Narkompros) (1918–19). Teacher and director of the Vitebsk School of Art (1919–22). Organiser of the Unovis (Affirmers of New Art) group. One of the main initiators in the creation of the Museum of Artistic Culture; director of the museum and then of the State Institute of Artistic Culture (Ginkhuk) in Petrograd/Leningrad

(1923–6). Taught at the Kiev Art Institute (1929–30) and in the House of the Arts (Dom Iskusstv) in Leningrad (1930). Headed the experimental laboratory at the State Russian Museum (1932–3).

From the mid 1910s, after Larionov's departure from Russia, Malevich became the recognised leader of the avant-garde movement. It was at this moment that he declared himself to be one of the leading Cubo-Futurists, and created Suprematism – an original pictorial system tending to Universalism which became one of the 'great utopias' of the Russian avant-garde. Malevich's works included here are significant and characteristic examples of this mature period in the artist's creative life, showing his Cubo-Futurism (*Portrait of I. V. Klyun*), 'alogizm' (*Cow and Violin*, alogizm being a combination of objects and words which Malevich advocated in 1913 – the period of his most fruitful collaboration with the Futurist poets who were developing similar motifs in their own work), and finally of Suprematism in its purest incarnation. [E.B.]

57 Alogizm (Cow and Violin), 1913 (p.6)
Oil on wood. 48·8 × 25·8 cm
Signed, inscribed and deliberately pre-dated by the artist on the back of the panel: *Аллогическое сопоставление двух форм "скрипка и корова" как момент борьбы с логизмом естественностью, мещанским смыслом и предрассудком. КМалевич 1911 год* [Allogistic comparison of two forms, a violin and a cow, as a moment of conflict with logizm through nature, vulgar thought and prejudice. KMalevich 1911]; label of the Museum of Artistic Culture; label inscribed: *№ 6 Малевич/М.Х.К./57/811* [No. 6 Malevich/Museum of Artistic Culture/57/811]
ЖБ-1550

At the exhibition *The Store* (Moscow, 1916), *Cow and Violin* was exhibited under the general heading *Алогизм форм 1913* [Alogizm of forms 1913]. This date can be regarded as more exact than that subsequently inscribed by the artist.

58 Portrait of I. V. Klyun (The Builder), 1913 (p.61)
Oil on canvas. 112 × 70 cm
Signed and deliberately pre-dated by the artist bottom left: *К Малевич 1911 г* [K Malevich 1911]; signed and inscribed by the artist on the back of the canvas: *Portrait de M-eur Klunkoff K. Malevitch 16 x 25 1/4*; labels: *Cimaise*; *2144*; label of the Museum of Artistic Culture
ЖБ-1469

A painting entitled *Portrait of Ivan Vasilievich Klyunkov* first appeared in the catalogue of the *Union of Youth* exhibition in 1912–13, but this was an earlier version of the present *Portrait* and its whereabouts are not now known (see ex. cat. of the *Malevich* exhibition; Leningrad, Moscow, Amsterdam, 1988–9. Ill. 16). The Russian Museum's *Portrait of I. V. Klyun*, an example of mature Cubo-Futurism, can be identified as the same painting as *Finished Portrait of Ivan Vasilievich Klyunkov* shown at the *Union of Youth* exhibition in 1913–14. This is confirmed by Alexander Benois' sketches in his copy of the catalogue, now kept in the manuscript section of the Russian Museum. As with *Cow and Violin*, the artist seems to have given the work an intentionally earlier date. This pre-dating attests to Malevich's attempt to redefine the starting date of his Cubo-Futurist period.

59 Red Square, 1915 (p.109)
Oil on canvas. 53 × 53 cm
Inscribed by the artist on the back of the canvas: *Крестьянка супрематуризм* [Peasant woman Suprematurism]; *684 12 x 12*; stamped: *МБ ИЗО* [MB IZO]; label of the Museum of Artistic Culture; inscribed by the artist on the stretcher: *Для журнала клише через сетку* [For the journal a cliché through a net]; label of the Anniversary Exhibition of 1932 with *No. 2341*
ЖБ-1643

Red Square was first exhibited at *The Last Futurist Exhibition of Paintings: 0.10* (Petrograd, 1915, No. 43) under the name *Pictorial Realism of a Peasant Woman in 2 Dimensions*. The artist's inscription on the back of the canvas gives one of the earliest variations of the name of his new movement: 'Suprematurism'.

60 Suprematism, 1915 (p.110)
Oil on canvas. 87·5 × 72 cm
Inscribed by the artist on the stretcher: *Н. Новгород* [Nizhny Novgorod]; inscribed on the back of the canvas: *464 М.Х.К.*; label of the Museum of Artistic Culture
ЖБ-1332

61 Suprematism (Supremus No. 58. Yellow and Black), 1915–16 (p.111)
Oil on canvas. 79·5 × 70·5 cm
Inscribed and signed by the artist on the back of the canvas: *Sup No. 58* (crossed out) *K.M 182 16 x 18*; label of the Museum of Artistic Culture; labels on the stretcher: *№ 42 Малевич* [No. 42 Malevich]; *№ 4084*; Anniversary Exhibition of 1932
ЖБ-1687

62 Self Portrait, 1908 (p.23)
Gouache, watercolour, Indian ink and varnish on paper. 46·2 × 41·3 cm
Stamped on the back of the passe-partout top left: *М.Б. ИЗО* [M.B. IZO]; *Малевич К.С. Автопортрет размер 10 x 10 инвентарной книге № 1901* [Malevich, K.S. Self Portrait dimensions 10 x 10 inventory book no. 1901]; label of the Museum of Artistic Culture
Р-56720

63 Still Life (Fruits), 1908 (p.22)
Watercolour and gouache on paper. 52·1 × 52·2 cm
Signed in graphite pencil bottom left: *Казимиръ Малевичъ* [Kazimir Malevich]
Р-8176

Ilya Ivanovich Mashkov
1881–1944

Painter. Studied at the Moscow School of Painting, Sculpture and Architecture (1900–9) under Abram Arkhipov, Leonid Pasternak, Konstantin Korovin and Valentin Serov. Founder-member of the Jack of Diamonds exhibiting society (1910), and participated in all its exhibitions. Took part in the World of Art exhibitions (1911–17, intermittently). In the 1900s and 1910s he made trips to Germany, France, England, Italy, Spain, Turkey and Egypt. From 1924 he was a member of the Association of Artists of Revolutionary Russia, and was one of the organisers of the Society of Moscow Artists (1927–8). Taught in his own studio (1904–17) and in the State Free Art Studios (Svomas), later the Higher Artistic and Technical Institute (Vkhutein) (1918–30). Managed the Central Studio of the Association of Artists of Revolutionary Russia (1925–9).

As with Konchalovsky, Mashkov's work provides a representative and instructive overview of the Jack of Diamonds group, which was characterised by its more moderate approach within the avant-garde movement. His paintings bear all the characteristic traits of the Jack of Diamonds artists, with their tendency towards a heightened, sometimes excessive, use of colour, an exaggerated sensual relationship to nature, and a brightly conveyed, vivacious mood of optimism. [E.B.]

64 Portrait of a Boy in a Painted Shirt, 1909 (p.27)
Oil on canvas. 119·5 × 80 cm
Signed top left: *Илья Машков* [Ilya Mashkov].
Inscribed on the back of the canvas: *вх. 107* [vkh. 107]; label with the artist's inscription: *Машков Илья Иванович Москва М Харитоновский пер. д. 4 кв7. тел. 4-11-23 Портрет мальчика в расписной рубашке. Размер – высота 27 верш. ширина – 20 верш. фактура – разная. Материал – масло. Грунт – белила, козеин. Год работы – март 1909* [Mashkov, Ilya Ivanovich, M. Kharitonovsky per., house 4, apartment 47, Tel. 4-11-23. *Portrait of a Boy in a Painted Shirt*. Size: height 27 vershoks [1 vershok = 4.4 cm], width 20 vershoks. Style – various. Material – oil. Priming – whitewash, casein. Year of work – March 1909]; exhibition label of the Jack of Diamonds group with *No. 49*; label of the Museum of Artistic Culture
ЖБ-1499

65 Winter City Landscape, *c.* 1914 (p. 26)
Oil on canvas. 89 × 86 cm
Signed bottom right: *И Машков* [I. Mashkov]; on the back of the
canvas: label of the Museum Office of the Fine Arts Department (IZO)
with *No. 1737*; label of the Museum of Artistic Culture
ЖБ-1718

Mikhail Vasilievich Matiushin
1861–1934

Painter, graphic artist, composer and art critic. Studied at the Moscow
Conservatory (1876–81), and played the violin in the Imperial Orchestra
in St Petersburg (1881–1913). Attended the drawing school of the
Society for the Encouragement of the Arts in St Petersburg (1894–8)
and studied at the Zvantseva School of Drawing and Painting (1902–5).
In 1900 he made a trip to Paris. Participated in exhibitions from 1909.
He was a founder-member of the Union of Youth group (1910) and
participated in its exhibitions (1911–14). In 1913 he composed the
music for the Futurist opera *Victory Over the Sun* (prologue by Velimir
Khlebnikov, libretto by Alexei Kruchenykh and sets by Malevich), and in
1916 the music to Kruchenykh's play *Conquered War*. Organised the
studio of Spatial Realism at the State Free Art Studios (Svomas) at the
Higher Artistic and Technical Workshops (Vkhutemas) (1918–26) and
directed the Department of Organic Culture at the State Institute of
Artistic Culture (Ginkhuk) in Petrograd/Leningrad (1923–6). The results
of his experiments were subsequently summarised in his publication
Spravochnik po tsvetu [*A Reference Book on Colour*, Moscow and
Leningrad, 1932]. Organiser of the *Zorved* ('see-know') group.

Movement in Space is probably Matiushin's central work, a fitting
epigraph to his entire creative output. Although he was one of the
leaders of the Russian avant-garde and inspired many of the innovative
projects created by the St Petersburg 'left', Matiushin the artist
produced comparatively few works. Multi-talented – musician, painter,
sculptor and art critic – and highly educated, Matiushin's greatest
achievement, perhaps, was as creator of the original theory of
'extended vision' which he definitively formulated at the beginning of
the 1920s and which became the basis of the activities of his *Zorved*
['see-know'] group. It was on the basis of this theory that he worked at
the Museum of Artistic Culture and then at the Department of Organic
Culture at the Petrograd State Institute of Artistic Culture (Ginkhuk).
At the heart of Matiushin's research lay the question of colour: man's
perception of colour in various conditions, the transmutability of colour
and forms in an environment, and the connection between visual, aural
and tactile functions in perception. As a rule, as in *Movement in Space*,
Matiushin studied the interaction of colour and the environment on
patterns of eight colours: reds, oranges, yellows, yellow-greens, light
blues, blues and violets. Based upon his 'Law of Supplementary
Colours' – the central principle of his theory – Matiushin divided his
colour scheme into a main active colour, an environmental background
colour, and a medium colour that brought them together. Matiushin
affirmed that colour is always mobile, that it relies upon adjoining
colours and upon the strength of the light and the extent of the colour
fields. His later research provided the basis for his *Spravochnik po
tsvety* (*Reference Book on Colour*; 1932). [O.Sh.]

66 Movement in Space, before 1922 (p. 117)
Oil on canvas. 124 × 168 cm
Initialled top right: *M.M.*
ЖБ-996

Kuzma Sergeevich Petrov-Vodkin
1878–1939

Painter, graphic artist, stage designer and art theorist. Studied at the
Samara School of Painting and Drawing under F. Burtsev (1894–5), the
Baron Stieglitz Central School for Technical Drawing (1895–7), the
Moscow School of Painting, Sculpture and Architecture (1897–1904)
under Abram Arkhipov, Nikolai Kasatkin and Valentin Serov, at the
Anton Ažbe school in Munich (1901), and in private studios in Paris

(1905–8). Travelled throughout Italy (1905–6) and North Africa (1907).
Took part in the following exhibitions: *Golden Fleece* (1908); *Union of
Russian Artists* (1909–10); *Heat-Colour* (1924); and others. Member of
the World of Art group (from 1910) and the Four Arts Society of Artists
(1925–8). Taught at the Zvantseva School of Drawing and Painting in St
Petersburg (from 1910), then at the Art School of the Academy of Arts
(1918–32).

In many ways Petrov-Vodkin, who continued in the Symbolist tradition
and adhered to classical norms, remained far removed both in his
creative and theoretical work from the issues that preoccupied the
representatives of the avant-garde. Nonetheless, he was very highly
considered in this circle as well. *Midday*, *Violin* and *Morning Still Life* are
undeniable masterpieces. Inherent in each is a genuinely philosophical
intonation. In his still lives, which the artist himself described as 'a
direct conversation between the painter and nature', Petrov-Vodkin
exhibits a profound understanding of the world around him. [E.B.]

67 Midday, 1917 (p. 59)
Oil on canvas. 89 × 128·5 cm
Artist's monogram and date bottom right: *КПВ 1917* [KPV 1917]
On the back of the canvas: label of the Museum of Artistic Culture
ЖБ-1263

68 Morning Still Life, 1918 (p. 57)
Oil on canvas. 66 × 88 cm
Artist's monogram and date bottom right: *1918-VII* [KPV 1918-VII]
On the stretcher: label with *Всекохудожник* [Vsekokhudozhnik]; label
with *013784 Петров-Водкин "Утренний натюрморт" 68 x 90* [013784
Petrov-Vodkin Morning Still Life 68 x 90 cm]; label of the First State
Free Art Exhibition, 1919 (torn); on the back of the canvas: label of the
Museum of Artistic Culture
ЖБ-2398

69 Violin, 1918 (p. 56)
Oil on canvas. 65 × 80 cm
Artist's monogram and date bottom right: *КПВ 1918-IV* [KPV 1918-IV]
On the stretcher: label with *Всекохудожник* [Vsekokhudozhnik]; label of
the First State Free Art Exhibition, 1919 (torn); label of the Anniversary
Exhibition of 1932; on the back of the canvas: label of the Museum of
Artistic Culture
ЖБ-1253

Liubov Sergeevna Popova
1889–1924

Painter, graphic artist and stage designer, also worked in the field of
decorative applied art. Studied in Stanislav Zhukovsky's studio in
Moscow (1907), in the Konstantin Yuon and I. Dudin School of Drawing
and Painting (1908–9) and at the Académie de La Palette in Paris under
Henri Le Fauconnier and Jean Metzinger (1912–13). Visited the Bashnya
['Tower'] studio in Moscow (1913). Travelled to Italy (1910). Took part in
the following exhibitions: *Jack of Diamonds* (1914, 1916); *Tramway V:
the First Futurist Exhibition of Paintings* (1915); *The Last Futurist
Exhibition of Paintings: 0.10* (1915); *The Store* (1916); and *5 x 5 = 25*
(1921). Was involved in the organisation of the Supremus society
(1916). Worked at the Institute of Artistic Culture (Inkhuk) in Moscow
(1920–4), and was also involved in the organisation of the Museum of
Artistic Culture (1921–2). Member of the LEF (Left Front of the Arts)
group (1922–4).

These three paintings by Popova are highly characteristic of her work in
the mid 1910s and mark the main stages in her creative evolution, from
a Cubist deconstruction of the objective world (*Portrait of a
Philosopher*) to pure abstraction. The name Popova gave to her
abstract pictures – *Painterly Architectonics* – underlines the structural
nature of her work and the monumentalism that was central to her
creative talent. [E.B]

70 Objects, 1915 (p.68)
Oil on canvas. 61 × 44·5 cm
Signed and inscribed by the artist on the stretcher: *Л. Попова
"Предметы" 1915 г. Москва Новиннский б. 117 д* [L. Popova *Objects*
1915. Moscow, Novinsky Boulevard, house 117]; on the back of the
canvas: label of the Museum of Artistic Culture
ЖБ-1636

71 Portrait of a Philosopher, 1915 (p.67)
Oil on Canvas. 89 × 63 cm
Signed on the stretcher: *Попова* [Popova]; inscribed by the artist on the
back of the canvas: *230 14 x 20*; label of the Museum of Artistic Culture
ЖБ-1456

72 Painterly Architectonics, 1916 (p.69)
Oil on canvas. 51 × 33 cm
Inscribed by the artist on the back of the canvas: *No. 229 11 1/4 x 7
1/2;* label of the Fine Arts Department (IZO); label of the Museum of
Artistic Culture
ЖБ-1635

Ivan Albertovich Puni (Jean Pougny)
1894–1956

Painter, graphic artist, stage designer, illustrator and art theorist.
Studied at the Military Academy in St Petersburg (1900–8). Travelled
to Italy, and then France where he studied in various studios, including
the Académie Julian in Paris (1910–12). Took part in the following
exhibitions: *Union of Youth* (1912–19); *Salon des Indépendants* (Paris,
1913–14); *Jack of Diamonds* (1916–17); *Four Arts Society of Artists*
(1928). One of the organisers of the Futurist exhibitions *Tramway V: the
First Futurist Exhibition of Paintings* (1915) and *The Last Futurist
Exhibition of Paintings: 0.10* (1915). Taught at the Petrograd State Free
Art Studios (1918) and the Vitebsk School of Art together with Chagall
(1919). Left Russia first for Berlin (1921) and then Paris (1923). In 1923
Puni wrote a critique of abstract art in his book *Contemporary Painting*
published in Berlin. His work abroad shows a return to figurative paint-
ing and an enduring enthusiasm for the work of Vuillard and Bonnard.
Puni's later, post-war paintings are distinguished by a heightened
expression of form and distinctive use of colour.

Puni painted *Portrait of the Artist's Wife* shortly after his return from
Paris and the painting clearly shows the artist's interest in the work of
the French Cubists. The picture was shown at the *Tramway V* Futurist
exhibition which Puni organised, and two years later at the *Jack of
Diamonds* exhibition. In *Portrait* Puni offers his own interpretation of
Cubism, which he enhances with musical rhythms of colour combina-
tions and unexpected juxtapositions of details. *Still Life with Letters,
Spectrum Flight* (1919) and *Violin* (1919) are clearly influenced by
Suprematism and are key works by Puni of that period. In a sense
Puni's version of Suprematism was compromised; he combined the
formulaic principles of Suprematism with real objects, words or
fragments of words, and various details of everyday life. In *Still Life with
Letters, Spectrum Flight* the verbal nature of the figurative composition
is self-evident. The work achieves its expressive force through
distinctive imitations revealing the interrelation of the word, the symbol
and its plastic metaphor. Thus, with the word *бегство* [flight] the letters
are randomly scattered across the canvas; the letters of *спектр*
[spectrum] rise to the surface of the canvas like the widening, focused
beam of a spotlight, while the word *форм* [forms] with its triple letter
'M' creates a sense of extended space. Later, in his one-man exhibition
at the Sturm-Galerie in Berlin (1921), Puni adapted this form of plastic
movement and displayed the word *бегство* on the walls of the
exhibition hall. He also repeated the work itself which, like *Violin*, he
could not take out of Russia. Although distinguished by an accentuated
aestheticism distinctive to Puni, *Violin* demonstrates more clearly than
the other works an adherence to Malevich's Suprematism. [O.Sh.]

73 Portrait of the Artist's Wife, 1914 (p.66)
Oil on canvas. 89 × 62·5 cm
Signed and dated bottom right: *Пуни 1914* [Puni 1914]
ЖБ-1627

74 Still Life with Letters, Spectrum Flight, 1919 (p.89)
Oil on canvas. 124 × 127 cm
Signed and dated bottom right: *И[в] Пуни 1919* [I(v). Puni. 1919]
ЖБ-2074

75 Violin, 1919 (p.88)
Oil on canvas. 115 × 145 cm
ЖБ-1339

Alexander Mikhailovich Rodchenko
1891–1956

Painter, graphic artist, sculptor and creator of spatial constructions,
photographer, designer and stage designer who also worked in
cinematography. Studied at the Kazan School of Art (1910–14) and the
Stroganov Central Art School in Moscow (1914–17). Took part in the
following exhibitions: *The Store* (1916); *Fifth, Tenth and Eleventh State
Exhibitions* (1919); *Obmokhu* (Society of Young Artists) (1920, 1921);
5 x 5 = 25 (1921); and the October group (1930). First one-man
exhibition in 1918. Member of the art collegium of the Fine Arts
Department (IZO) of the People's Commissariat for Enlightenment
(Narkompros), and head of the Museum Office and a member of its
first purchasing committee (1918–21); founder-member of the Institute
of Artistic Culture in Moscow (Inkhuk; 1920–4) where, in 1921, he
succeeded Kandinsky as chairman of the presidium and became one
of the organisers of the Institute's Working Group of Constructivists.
In 1925, at the *Exposition Internationale des Arts Décoratifs* in Paris, he
was acclaimed for his Workers' Club project. He taught at the Moscow
Proletkult (Proletarian Culture) school (1918), at the woodwork and
metal-processing faculties of the Higher Artistic and Technical
Workshops (Vkhutemas; 1920–30), and gave courses in photography at
the Moscow Polygraphic Institute (1930s). In the 1920s he collaborated
with the periodicals *Lef*, *Kinofot* and *Ogonyok*, and worked a great deal
on agit-posters and in the field of advertising. In the 1930s he worked
primarily with the magazine *SSSR na stroyke* ['USSR in Construction'].
From the mid 1920s until 1942 he worked mostly in photography,
though in 1938 he returned to painting.

These works by Rodchenko date to a brief but highly productive period
in the artist's creative life. It was during these years (1918–22) that
Rodchenko completed his series of paintings and drawings entitled
Dynamism of Surface, *Concentration of Colour*, *Linearism*, *Black on
Black*, *Smooth Colour* and others, as well as three series of spatial constructions demonstrating an original approach to abstract painting.
Construction, *Abstract Composition*, *White Circle* and *Black on Black*
are abstract compositions differentiated by the simplest geometric
forms, through which the artist constructs a new graphic spatiality. Line,
colour and space are the main components of Rodchenko's painting.
The composition *Black on Black*, a response to Malevich's work *White
on White*, deserves special attention. The work's multiplicity of textures
enabled the artist to create in monochrome a sense of spatial depth.
The essence of Rodchenko's art is experimentation. In 1921 he
'brought [painting] to its logical conclusion', when, at the *5 x 5 = 25*
exhibition, he exhibited three canvases – in yellow, blue and red.
Rodchenko subsequently abandoned painting for a time, instead
channelling all his earlier experience into design, spatial constructions,
architecture and photomontage. [O.Sh.]

'To create something new you need a new means of expression', wrote
Rodchenko in 1920. 'Today's impetuousness will always hide deep
within itself the painstaking pedantry of technique. From 1915
Rodchenko began to work on compositions in which lines described
with the aid of a pair of compasses and ruler play a central role. In 1919
he also introduced the ruler and compasses into his engravings, stating
that the line was an independent form in painting and an independent
element of construction. Each sheet in the album *Rodchenko's
Engravings, 1919* represents a finished composition made up of circles,
either one inside another, adjoining each other or intersecting, and
broken up or pierced with lines. The album dates to his early work
using lines as a main structural element. Here there is a tendency

towards excess and dynamism which by 1920 was replaced by more schematic constructions. With these later works Rodchenko also combined geometric forms with various surface textures. He observed how identical shapes could create different spatial impressions according to how they were worked – smooth or rough textures, highly coloured or lit, compared or contrasted. *Abstract Composition* dates to the period of his highly significant *Linearism* cycle. The colour and particular intricacy of this drawing's composition emphasise not only the constructive, but also the decorative possibilities of line. In 1921 Rodchenko summarised his experiments in *Line*, a brochure written for the Institute of Artistic Culture. [L.V.]

76 **Construction**, 1917 (p.90)
Oil on wood. 73 × 32 cm
Inscribed in brown paint on the back of the panel: *Родченко. 1917* [Rodchenko. 1917]; in pencil: *No. 28 321/2 x 73*
ЖБ-1552

77 **Abstract Composition**, 1918 (p.92)
Oil on wood. 53 × 21 cm
Inscribed in white paint on a black rectangle on the back of the canvas: *Родченко* [Rodchenko]; in black: *1918 г.* [1918]
ЖБ-1649

78 **Black on Black**, 1918 (p.93)
Oil on canvas. 84 × 66·5 cm
Inscribed in black paint on the back of the canvas: *Родченко 1918* [Rodchenko 1918]
ЖБ-1437

79 **White Circle**, 1918 (p.91)
Oil on canvas. 89·2 × 71·5 cm
Inscribed bottom right: *P. 18* [R.18]
Inscribed in green paint on the back of the canvas: *Родченко 1918* [Rodchenko. 1918]
ЖБ-1439

80 **Title Page**, 1919
Linocut. 15·8 × 10·7 cm
Graphite-pencil inscription top right: *7*; beneath illustration on passe-partout: *Родченко. 1919 г* [Rodchenko 1919]
Crp-532

81 **Composition of Geometric Figures**, 1919
Linocut. 15·8 × 10·7 cm
Graphite-pencil inscription beneath illustration: *8*; beneath illustration on passe-partout: *Родченко. 1919 г* [Rodchenko 1919]
Crp-533

82 **Composition**, 1919
Linocut. 15·8 × 10·8 cm
Graphite-pencil inscription beneath illustration: *6*; beneath illustration on passe-partout: *Родченко. 1919 г* [Rodchenko 1919]
Crp-534

83 **Composition**, 1919
Linocut. 15·7 × 10·6 cm
Graphite-pencil inscription beneath illustration: *1*; beneath illustration on passe-partout: *Родченко. 1919 г* [Rodchenko 1919]
Crp-535

84 **Composition**, 1919
Linocut. 15·7 × 10·7 cm
Graphite-pencil inscriptionl beneath illustration: *5*; beneath illustration on passe-partout: *Родченко. 1919 г* [Rodchenko 1919]
Crp-536

85 **Composition**, 1919
Linocut. 15·8 × 10·6 cm
Graphite-pencil inscription beneath illustration: *11*; beneath illustration on passe-partout: *Родченко. 1919 г* [Rodchenko 1919]
Crp-537

86 **Composition**, 1919
Linocut. 15·7 × 10·7 cm
Graphite-pencil inscription beneath illustration: *4*; beneath illustration on passe-partout: *Родченко. 1919 г* [Rodchenko 1919]
Crp-538

87 **Composition**, 1919
Linocut. 15·7 × 10·6 cm
Graphite-pencil inscription beneath illustration: *9*; beneath illustration on passe-partout: *Родченко. 1919 г* [Rodchenko 1919]
Crp-539

88 **Composition**, 1919
Linocut. 15·7 × 11 cm
Graphite-pencil inscription beneath illustration: *2*; beneath illustration on passe-partout: *Родченко. 1919 г* [Rodchenko 1919]
Crp-540

89 **Composition**, 1919
Linocut. 17·2 × 11·4 cm
Graphite-pencil inscription beneath illustration: *9*; beneath illustration on passe-partout: *Родченко. 1919 г* [Rodchenko 1919]
Crp-541

90 **Composition**, 1919
Linocut. 19·2 × 11·2 cm
Graphite-pencil inscription beneath illustration: *12*; beneath illustration on passe-partout: *Родченко. 1919 г* [Rodchenko 1919]
Crp-542

91 **Composition**, 1919
Linocut. 15·7 × 10·2 cm
Graphite-pencil inscription beneath illustration: *10*; beneath illustration on passe-partout: *Родченко. 1919 г* [Rodchenko 1919]; top right: *7*; on the back of the passe-partout in ink: *Родченко. 4.000 p* [Rodchenko. 4,000 roubles]
Crp-543

92 **Composition**, 1919
Linocut. 15·7 × 11·1 cm
Graphite-pencil inscription beneath illustration: *2*; beneath illustration on passe-partout: *Родченко. 1919 г* [Rodchenko 1919]; on the back of the passe-partout in ink: *Родченко. 4.000 p* [Rodchenko. 4,000 roubles]
Crp-544

93 **Abstract Drawing**, 1921
Coloured and graphite pencil on paper. 37 × 29·1 cm
Signed and dated in graphite pencil bottom right: *Родченко I IV 21* [Rodchenko I.IV.21]; inscribed in graphite pencil on the back: *Родченко. M.X.K. 526* [Rodchenko Museum of Artistic Culture 526]
Срб-105

Nicholas Roerich (Nikolai Konstantinovich Rerikh)
1874–1947

Painter, graphic artist and stage designer. Studied at the Faculty of Law at St Petersburg University, the Academy of Arts (1893–9) under Arkhip Kuindzhi and at Fernand Cormon's studio in Paris (1900). Travelled around ancient Russian towns (1903–4). Member of the World of Art group (from 1899, chairman from 1910) and the Union of Russian Artists (1903–10). Worked as a stage designer for Diaghilev's theatrical productions (1908–14). In 1918 he emigrated and went to live in the USA (1920–2) and then India (from 1923).

Although he was one of the leading artists of the World of Art group, Roerich did not belong to the avant-garde movement. *Sacred Island*, the only painting by Roerich to be transferred from the Fine Arts Department (IZO) to the Museum of Artistic Culture, was there more by chance than design. This is confirmed in a memorandum by V. Yermolaeva in April 1925, which refers to the works of Roerich and

Kustodiev as 'not intended for the Museum of Artistic Culture'. [E.B.]

94 Sacred Island, 1917 (p.58)
Tempera on canvas. 49 × 77 cm
On the stretcher: label of the First State Free Art Exhibition, 1919, with *No. 1171*; label of the Fine Arts Department (IZO) with *No. 199/4*; on the back of the canvas: label of the Museum of Artistic Culture
Ж-5503

Olga Vladimirovna Rozanova
1886–1918

Painter, graphic artist, illustrator of Futurist books and art theorist. Studied at the Stroganov Central Art School in Moscow (1904–10) and at the Zvantseva School of Drawing and Painting in St Petersburg (1911). Took part in the following exhibitions: *Union of Youth* (1911–14); the *International Futurist Exhibition* (Rome, 1914); *Tramway V: the First Futurist Exhibition of Paintings* (1915); *The Last Futuristic Exhibition of Paintings: 0.10* (1915); *The Store* (1916); and *Jack of Diamonds* (1916, 1917). Member of the Supremus group founded by Malevich (1916). Member of the Fine Arts Department (IZO) of the People's Commissariat for Enlightenment (Narkompros), and of Proletkult (Proletarian Cultural Organisation) (1918), where she headed the applied art section.

Olga Rozanova was highly regarded by her contemporaries, and recognised in her short lifetime as one of the central figures of the Russian avant-garde. Her paintings included here date to the high point of her creative life, showing her progression from early Neo-Primitive (essentially Fauvist) works such as *Red House* and *The Smithy*, and her subsequent interest in Cubo-Futurism (*Writing Desk*), to abstract art in its Suprematist form. However, it is clear that Rozanova's style differs significantly from Malevich's Suprematism: her decorative, richly illuminated style of painting – which Rozanova herself called 'transformed colouring' – prevails over the ideological, religious basis of Suprematism. [E.B.]

95 Red House, 1910 (p.30)
Oil on canvas. 85 × 98 cm
Inscribed on the back: *340 19 1/2 Е 22 3/4 Ольга Розанова* [340 19 1/2 x 22 3/4 Olga Rozanova]; label of the Museum of Artistic Culture
ЖБ-1481

96 The Smithy, 1912 (p.33)
Oil on canvas. 90 × 98 cm
On the back of the canvas: label of the First State Free Art Exhibition, 1919, with *No. 1180*; label of the Fine Arts Department (torn); label of the Museum of Artistic Culture
ЖБ-1322

97 In a Café, 1912–13 (p.32)
Oil on canvas. 61 × 83 cm
Inscribed on the back of the canvas: *460 14 x 18 3/4*; label with *No. 52*; label of the Museum of Artistic Culture
ЖБ-1614

98 Writing Desk, 1916 (p.73)
Oil on canvas. 66 × 49 cm
Monogram bottom left
Inscribed on the back of the canvas: *460 15 x 11*; label with *No. 87*; label of the Museum of Artistic Culture
ЖБ-1615

99 Non-Objective Composition (Suprematism), c. 1916 (p.112)
Oil on canvas. 62·5 × 40·5 cm
Inscribed on the back of the canvas: *314 14 x 9*; *О Розанова* [314 14 x 9; O. Rozanova; No. 104]; stamped: *М.Б. ИЗО* [M.B. IZO]; label of the Museum of Artistic Culture
ЖБ-1579

100 Non-Objective Composition (Suprematism), c. 1916 (p.113)
Size paint on canvas. 58 × 44 cm
Inscribed on the back of the canvas: *315 10 x 13*; stamped: *М.Б. ИЗО* [M.B. IZO]; label of the Museum of Artistic Culture
ЖБ-1638

101 Non-Objective Composition (Suprematism), c. 1916 (p.115)
Oil on canvas. 85 × 60·5 cm
Inscribed on the back of the canvas: *454 13 1/2 x 19*; label with *No. 111*; label of the Museum of Artistic Culture
ЖБ-1360

102 Non-Objective Composition (Suprematism), c. 1916 (p.114)
Oil on canvas. 78·5 × 53 cm
Inscribed on the back of the canvas: *306 18 x 12*; label of the Museum of Artistic Culture
ЖБ-1382

Sergei Yakovlevich Senkin
1894–1963

Painter, graphic artist and designer. Studied at the Moscow School of Painting, Sculpture and Architecture (1914–15) and at the State Free Art Studios under Malevich (1918–19, 1920). In 1920, together with Gustav Klutsis, he opened his own independent workshop in the Higher Artistic and Technical Workshops (Vkhutemas). Took part in exhibitions of the Unovis (Affirmers of New Art) group at the Cézanne Students' Club in Moscow (1921, 1922), and the Union of New Tendencies in Art (1922, Petrograd). In 1923, Senkin, together with Klutsis, opened the Workshop of the Revolution at Vkhutemas. From 1921 he lived in Vitebsk. From 1923 he worked with *Lef* magazine. From 1928 he was a member of the October group. During these years he worked with El Lissitzky on photomontages for the *Press* exhibition in Cologne (1928). In 1923 he exhibited a project at the Central Institute of Labour department of the All-Russian Agricultural exhibition. Subsequently he worked mainly in the field of photomontage.

Sergei Senkin is little known today and his artistic legacy is extremely small. A pupil of Malevich, Senkin developed his teacher's ideas, working for about two to three years in the style of geometric abstraction. In 1921 he showed thirty works – Suprematist paintings and Suprematist spatial models – at the Cézanne Club, which, judging by the surviving examples, were stylistically close to the Suprematist compositions of Malevich. These works from the State Russian Museum therefore signify a new direction in Senkin's creative quest. Here he employs a more restrained colour palette for his *Suprematist Compositions*, shades of black, white and grey predominating. Central to these compositions is their multi-layered structure: the translucence of the geometrical surfaces that form the composition creates the effect of one form merging into the next. Senkin evidently varied this graphic device several times, often, as here, using glass as a basis for the painting, then achieving a similar result on canvas. It is possible that these compositions were influenced to some extent by the work of Klutsis, with whom Senkin collaborated actively over these years. [O.Sh.]

103 Suprematist Composition,* 1922 (p.106)
Oil on canvas. 37 × 45 cm
Initialled bottom right: *CC* [SS]
Inscribed on the back of the canvas: *С. Сенькин 22* [S. Senkin 22]
ЖС-65
* Called *Study* in the transfer document from the Museum of Artistic Culture

104 Suprematist Composition,* 1922 (p.105)
Oil on glass backed with cardboard. 36·5 × 28 cm
Inscribed in red paint on the back of the cardboard: *С. Сенькин 1922* [S. Senkin 1922]; in black: *No.2*
ЖС-66
* Called *Study* in the transfer document from the Museum of Artistic Culture

Iosif Solomonovich Shkolnik
1883–1926

Painter and stage designer. Graduated from the Odessa School of Art (1905). Studied at the Academy of Arts in St Petersburg (1905–7). Participated in the *Triangle* exhibition (1909). One of the organisers and an active member of the Union of Youth (1910–14) as its secretary and editor of a number of publications. Worked on the staging of the tragedy *Vladimir Mayakovsky* (1913). Member of the collegium of the Fine Arts Department of the People's Commissariat for Enlightenment (1918); director of its stage design section, which in 1920 became the Design Institute. Professorial head of the stage design class of the Petrograd State Free Art Studios (from 1919).

Despite his active participation in the Union of Youth, Shkolnik was never one of the leaders of the avant-garde. Nevertheless, significant features of the avant-garde movement as a whole are reflected in his creative work: his experiments with colour, the emphatically decorative nature of his painting style and his interest in folk art which was so characteristic of many other artists of the avant-garde. [E.B.]

105 Landscape, early 1910s (p.44)
Size paint on canvas. 50 × 68·3 cm
On the back of the canvas: label of the First State Free Art Exhibition, 1919, with *No. 1596*; label of the Museum of Artistic Culture with the inscription: *№ 34 Не приобретено для М.Х.К.* [No. 34. Not acquired for the Museum of Artistic Culture]
ЖС-67

106 The Provinces, early 1910s (p.44)
Size paint on canvas. 70·5 × 88·5 cm
Ж-9520

David Petrovich Shterenberg
1881–1948

Painter, graphic artist and book illustrator. Studied fine art in a private studio in Odessa in 1905, and in 1906 continued his artistic education in Vienna, and then in Paris at the Académie Vitti (1907–12) under Professor A. Martenet, Kees van Dongen and E. Anglada, living in 'La Ruche' where Modigliani, Chagall, Soutine and many others stayed at various times. In Paris Shterenberg also associated with such artists as Marquet, Ozenfant, Léger, Utrillo and Bonnard, and the poet Apollinaire. In 1914 he made a brief visit to Russia to organise his exhibition in Kiev. He returned to Russia in 1917. From 1912 he took part in the exhibitions of the Spring and Autumn Salons and the *Salon des Indépendants*. In 1917 his work was included in a group exhibition in Paris along with that of Matisse, Ozenfant and Utrillo; and in 1922 in the 'Exhibition of the Three' (with Altman and Chagall) in Moscow. From 1925 to 1930 he was a founder-member and chairman of the Society of Easel Painters (OST). From 1917 to 1919 he was commissar for the arts, and director (1918–20) of the Fine Arts Department of the People's Commissariat for Enlightenment. In the 1920s he was a member of the Jewish cultural association, the Cultural League. From 1920 to 1930 he was a professor at the Higher Artistic and Technical Workshops, then Institute (Vkhutemas/Vkhutein) in Moscow. In 1925 he was director of the Soviet section at the *Exposition Internationale des Arts Décoratifs* in Paris. In 1928 he was a member and correspondent of the Union of German Book Illustrators; the same year he worked in the State Jewish Theatre and the Moscow Theatre (formerly the 'Korsh'). He was awarded the title of Honoured Artist in 1930. In 1932 he became the first deputy chairman of the newly-created Moscow Society of Artists. From 1924 to 1944 he worked on the 'Tass windows'. After 1930 he was primarily an illustrator of children's books.

Shterenberg's work is represented here by his still lives, a genre in which he worked with great success in the years immediately following the Revolution. Paintings such as *Still Life with Cherries*, *Sponge and Soap* and *Table and Fir Tree* can be seen as the completion of an earlier stage in the artist's evolution, which led him from Impressionism to Cubism. Despite his subsequent peripheral involvement with Futurism and its analysis of movement, Shterenberg became a firm opponent of abstract painting. In his still lives Shterenberg focuses not so much on the objects themselves, as on the interrelationships between them. Transforming the three-dimensionality of the outside world to the demands of a two-dimensional painting, the artist freely combines techniques of abstract painting with the totally concrete depiction of objects. This distinctive synthesis of the depiction of reality

and conventional totality with a sharpness of compositional solutions shows a certain special, refined artistry. Interested in finding different ways of conveying meaning through texture, Shterenberg experimented with a variety of techniques: at times he applied paint to the canvas as delicately as if it were water-colour; at others so thickly that it takes on the quality of relief. The artist often used a palette-knife instead of a brush; he would apply paint with his finger, pattern it with a comb, or press patterned convex objects into the wet surface of the painting. However, this experimentation with texture was not an end in itself for Shterenberg, whose still lives, in the words of the critic Yankov Tugendkhold, 'combine a technical appreciation of form…with a psychological understanding of content'. [O.Sh.]

107 Still Life with Cherries, *1919 (p.83)
Oil on canvas. 68 × 67 cm
Signed bottom left: *Д. Штеренберг* [D. Shterenberg]
ЖБ-1540
* Called *Still Life with Plate* in the transfer document from the Museum of Artistic Culture

108 Sponge and Soap, 1920 (p.82)
Oil on canvas. 46 × 61 cm
ЖБ-1574

109 Table and Fir Tree, early 1920s (p.80)
Oil on canvas. 142·3 × 102 cm
Inscribed in black paint on the back of the canvas: *Д. П. Штеренберг* [D. P. Shterenberg]; in red paint: *МЕНЮ!* [MENU!]
ЖБ-1335

Vladimir Avgustovich Stenberg
1899–1982

Painter, graphic artist, sculptor, designer, architect and stage designer. From 1912 to 1917 he studied at the Stroganov Central Art School and at the stage-design department of the State Free Art Studios (Svomas) together with his brother G. Stenberg, V. Komardenkov, K. Medunetsky, S. Svetlov, N. Denisovsky and others. Took part in exhibitions from 1919. Organiser and member of the Society of Young Artists (Obmokhu; 1919–23). In 1921, together with his brother and Medunetsky, he organised the Constructivists exhibition at the Poets' Café in Moscow. From 1920 he was a member of the Institute of Artistic Culture (Inkhuk) where, in 1921, he joined the First Working Group of Constructivists and participated in the creation of the 'Constructivism Laboratory'. From 1922 to 1931 he designed sets for productions at the Kamerny Theatre. He was a member of the LEF group from 1923 to 1925. From 1923 he worked on cinema posters. Taught at the Moscow Architecture and Construction Institute (1929–32). From 1928 he worked on the decorations in Red Square celebrating the anniversary of the Revolution, and subsequently (1940–1970) he worked primarily on decorations for celebrations and state ceremonies in Moscow.

Stenberg was one of the leaders of the Society of Young Artists (Obmokhu) and his work shows all the central features of the Constructivist movement. To the uninitiated eye *Colour Construction No. 4* is reminiscent of a plan or map. The interest in technique, suggested in the title, is clearly at the heart of Stenberg's creative work, inspired by the desire 'to construct through pictorial means a graphic modulus of the aesthetic environment of the future'. It is interesting that Stenberg uses similar plastic elements for his spatial constructions in wood and metal. Like many artists of his generation, Stenberg gave aesthetic qualities to a plan or map, and found beauty in the plastic details of machines or in the metal design of exposed constructions. Such experiments subsequently found a direct outlet in design, in architecture and other forms of visual agitation; they also significantly enhanced the expressive possibilities of stage design. [O.Sh.]

110 Colour Construction No. 4,* 1920 (p.107)
Oil on canvas. 75 × 38·5 cm
Inscribed on the back of the canvas: *В. Стенберг. 1920 г. Цвето-конструкция № 4* [V. Stenberg. 1920 *Colour Construction No. 4* 17 x 9]
ЖБ-1645
* Called *Light Construction No. 4* in the transfer document from the Museum of Artistic Culture

111 Abstract Composition, 1920
Indian ink and whitening on paper. 30·4 × 18·5 cm
Initialled in Indian ink bottom right: *Г. СТ.* [G. ST]; on the back in Indian ink: *ГЕОРГИЙ СТЕНБЕРГ/2/1920 г* [GEORGY STENBERG/2/1920]; stamp of the Museum Office of the Fine Arts Department of Narkompros, number 2596, Moscow
Срб-166

Varvara Feodorovna Stepanova
(sometimes worked under the pseudonyms *VarSt* and *Agarykh*)
1894–1958

Painter, textile designer and graphic artist. Studied at the Kazan School of Art where she met Rodchenko (1911–13). Studied at the art studio of Konstantin Yuon in Moscow (1913). and at the Stroganov Central Art School (1913–14). She worked with Rodchenko in the Museums Office of the Fine Arts Department (IZO) of the People's Commissariat for Enlightenment (Narkompros) as assistant director in the art and literature section (1918–23). Member of the presidium of the art section in the Fine Arts department of Rabis (Trade Union of Art Workers) (1920–3). Member of the General Working Group of Objective Analysis at the Institute of Artistic Culture (Inkhuk) (1920) and a founder-member of the First Working Group of Constructivists at the same institute (1921). She participated in the *5 x 5 = 25* exhibition (Moscow, 1921). Taught in the fine arts department of the Academy of Communist Education (1921–35). Took part in the First Russian Art Exhibition at the Van Diemen Gallery in Berlin (1932). She made sketches of costumes and sets for Meyerhold's staging of *Smert Tarelkina* ['The Death of Tarelkin'] (1922). She also made sketches of drawings for the First State Textile Print Factory (1923–5) and taught at the Textile Faculty of the Higher Artistic and Technical Institute (Vkhutemas) (1924–8). She designed books and collaborated with the journals *Lef* (1923–8) and *Novy Lef* (1926–32). Worked with Rodchenko on the journal *SSSR na stroyke* ['USSR in Construction'] (1930).

From 1919 to 1921 Stepanova was preoccupied by the question of form. It was at this time that her series of drawings and paintings entitled *Figures* appeared. She set out to create images using structural forms, and constructed figures from the simplest geometric forms, neither fully representational nor fully abstract. Stepanova believed that experiments were key to her objective artistic merit. Her linocuts, which are printed on coloured paper, are also – like the paintings of this series – based upon the play of contrasting textures, such as a matt or rough surface, a layer of paint, glossy or shiny paper surfaces. [L.V.]

112 Illustration on the Cover of a Folder, 1919 (p.94)
Linocut on black paper. 6·5 × 11·5 cm
On the back of the top flap of the folder in coloured pencil: *384*; in graphite pencil: *(МХК)/(15шт)/Степанова* [(Museum of Artistic Culture)/(15 pieces)/Stepanova]
Crp-6854

113 Composition of Two Figures, Male and Female, Against a Circle, 1919 (p.94)
Linocut on red paper. 16·7 × 11·5 cm
Signed bottom right of passe-partout in coloured pencil: *ВарСт* [VarSt]
Crp-6855

114 Composition of Two Figures, Male and Female, 1919 (p.94)
Linocut on grey paper. 11·5 × 9·5 cm
Signed bottom right of passe-partout in coloured pencil: *ВарСт* [VarSt]
Crp-6856

115 Human Figure Composed of Geometric Planes, 1919 (p.94)
Linocut on blue paper. 14·5 × 10 cm
Signed bottom right of passe-partout in coloured pencil: *ВарСт* [VarSt]
Crp-6857

116 Human Figure Composed of Geometric Planes, 1919 (p.94)
Linocut on red paper. 15 × 10·5 cm
Signed bottom right of passe-partout in coloured pencil: *ВарСт* [VarSt]
Crp-6858

117 Composition of Two Figures: Male Composed of Rectangles; Female Composed of Ovals, 1919 (p.95)
Linocut on blue paper. 17 × 11·5 cm
Signed bottom right of passe-partout in coloured pencil: *ВарСт* [VarSt]
Crp-6859

118 Composition of Four Figures: Male, Female and Two Children, 1919 (p.95)
Linocut on pink paper. 12·5 × 16·2 cm
Signed bottom right of passe-partout in coloured pencil: *ВарСт* [VarSt]
Crp-6860

119 Composition of Two Figures: Male Composed of Rectangles; Female Composed of Ovals, 1919 (p.95)
Linocut on blue paper. 12·5 × 16·4 cm
Signed bottom right of passe-partout in coloured pencil: *ВарСт* [VarSt]
Crp-6861

120 Human Figure Composed of Geometric Planes, 1919 (p.94)
Linocut on green paper. 13 × 7 cm
Signed bottom right of passe-partout in coloured pencil: *ВарСт* [VarSt]
Crp-6862

121 Female Figure Composed of Triangles and Circles, 1919 (p.94)
Linocut on black paper. 17 × 10·2 cm
Signed bottom right of passe-partout in coloured pencil: *ВарСт* [VarSt]
Crp-6863

122 Figure of a Seated Man Composed of Geometric Planes, 1919 (p.94)
Linocut on blue paper. 21·5 × 14 cm
Signed bottom right of passe-partout in coloured pencil: *ВарСт* [VarSt]
Crp-6864

123 Human Figure Composed of Ovals and Interconnecting Lines, 1919 (p.94)
Linocut on red paper. 16·9 × 10·7 cm
Signed bottom right of passe-partout in coloured pencil: *ВарСт* [VarSt]
Crp-6865

124 Composition of Two Human Figures Composed of Interconnecting Lines, 1919 (p.95)
Linocut on grey paper. 14·5 × 13·8 cm
Signed bottom right of passe-partout in coloured pencil: *ВарСт* [VarSt]
Crp-6866

125 Composition of Two Human Figures Composed of Intersecting Lines, 1919 (p.95)
Linocut on white paper. 14·5 × 13·8 cm
Signed bottom right of passe-partout in coloured pencil: *ВарСт* [VarSt]
Crp-6867

126 Standing Figure Composed of Geometric Planes, 1919 (p.95)
Linocut on grey paper. 10·4 × 9·5 cm
Signed bottom right of passe-partout in coloured pencil: *ВарСт* [VarSt]
Crp-6868

127 Composition of Geometric Planes, 1919 (p.95)
Linocut on blue paper. 10·8 × 7·5 cm
Signed bottom right of passe-partout in coloured pencil: *ВарСт* [VarSt]
Crp-6869

Vladislav Maximilianovich Strzeminsky
1883–1952

Painter, graphic artist, stage designer, art critic and theorist. Studied at the Nikolaevsky Military Engineering School in St Petersburg (1911–14) and at the State Free Art Studios (Svomas) in Moscow (1918–19). He was influenced by Malevich, and took his ideas to Poland. Took part in exhibitions from 1919. Wounded in the First World War and lost his left arm and right leg. Collegium member of the Fine Arts Department of the People's Commissariat for Enlightenment in Moscow (1918–19). Taught at Svomas in Smolensk; with Katarzyna Kobro organised the local affiliation of Unovis (Affirmers of New Art; 1919–21). Left for Poland in 1922 and joined the Block group (1924–6) and the Praesens group

(1926–9). Organiser and leader of the group *A.r* (1929–35). Wrote *Unism in Painting* (1928), the theory behind the Unism movement, which he created. One of the initiators in the founding of the Museum of Contemporary Art in Lodz, where he lived from 1931.

Still Life is one of the few surviving early works by Strzeminsky. It dates to the brief period when he was studying at the State Free Art Studios in Moscow. However, for Strzeminsky his true and formative education came from contact with the leaders of the avant-garde. The Russian period of his creative life, which lasted only a few years (1918–21), was marked by significant achievements and made a lasting influence on the future leader of the Polish avant-garde. *Still Life* bears the unmistakable influence of Malevich, while *Tools and Factory Goods* – a composition which combines easel painting and relief – is reminiscent of the Constructivists, and, above all, the counter-reliefs of Tatlin. [O.Sh.]

128 Still Life, 1919 (p.100)
Oil and mixed media on plywood. 38·2 × 26 cm
Inscribed in red ink on the back of the plywood: *№ 14 кв № 23* [No.14 receipt no.23]; label of the Museum of Artistic Culture
ЖБ-1389

129 Tools and Factory Goods, 1920 (p.101)
Oil on canvas backed by board, with cork, tin-plate, metal details and gypsum. 44·5 × 33 cm
Inscribed on the back of the board: *Стржеминский* [Strzeminsky]; label of the Museum Fund with *No. 345*; label of the Museum of Artistic Culture
ЖБ-1665

Vladimir Evgrafovich Tatlin
1885–1953

Painter, graphic artist, stage designer, monumentalist, constructor and author of architectural and engineering projects. Studied at the Penza School of Art (1904–10), the Moscow School of Painting, Sculpture and Architecture (1902–3 and 1909–10) under Valentin Serov and Konstantin Korovin. Served in the navy (1902–4) and as a merchant sea cadet went to Syria, Turkey, Morocco, Greece, Italy and other countries. Visited Berlin and Paris (1913). Took part in the following exhibitions: *Donkey's Tail* (1912), *Jack of Diamonds* (1913), *Union of Youth* (1910–14), *Tramway V: The First Futurist Exhibition of Paintings* (1915), *The Last Futurist Exhibition: 0.10* (1915) and *The Store* (1916). Member of the Union of New Tendencies in Art (1922–3). Chairman of the Left Federation of the Moscow Union of Artists (1917), director of the Moscow Committee of the Fine Arts Department of the People's Commissariat for Enlightenment (1918–19). One of the most active initiators in the creation of the Museum of Artistic Culture and the State Institute of Artistic Culture (Ginkhuk) where he headed the Department of Material Culture. Taught widely in Petrograd, Kiev and Moscow. Directed the Experimental Laboratory at the People's Commissariat for Enlightenment (1929–32).

Tatlin's self-portrait, *Sailor*, is a particularly important work that belongs to a relatively early period in the artist's creative life. However, it already shows features instantly recognisable in Tatlin's work: a style that is laconic, at times impetuous, and highly expressive. It is difficult to place Tatlin's style of painting within any particular movement in Russian art of the time; indeed, in 1915 the artist himself openly denied allegiance to any one movement: 'I have never belonged to Tatlinism, Rayism, Futurism or to the Peredvizhniki [Wanderers], and I never shall.' [E.B.]

130 Sailor, 1911 (p.43)
Tempera on canvas. 71·5 × 71·5 cm
Signed and inscribed by the artist on the back of the canvas: *B.E. Татлинь "Матросъ"* [V. E. Tatlin. *Sailor*]; label of the Museum of Artistic Culture
ЖБ-1514

Nadezhda Andreevna Udaltsova
1886–1961

Painter and graphic artist. Studied in Moscow at the private studios of Konstantin Yuon (1905) and Istvan Kiss (1909), then in Paris (together with Popova and Pestel) at the Académie de La Palette under Henri Le Fauconnier and Jean Metzinger. Visited Tatlin's 'Bashnya' [Tower] studio in Moscow (1913) where she worked with Tatlin and Alexander Vesnin. Took part in the following exhibitions: *Jack of Diamonds* (1914, 1916), *Tramway V: The First Futurist Exhibition of Paintings* (1915), *The Last Futurist Exhibition: 0.10* (1915), *The Store* (1916), and others. Joined the Supremus group (1916–17). Member of the Moscow Committee of the Fine Arts Department of the People's Commissariat for Enlightenment (1918). Taught at the Higher Artistic and Technical Workshops, later Institute (Vkhutemas/Vkhutein; 1920–30). Worked at the Institute of Artistic Culture (Inkhuk; 1920–1). Member of the Society of Moscow Painters (1925) and the Society of Moscow Artists (1927–8).

Among the artists of her generation, Udaltsova was the most receptive to French Cubism, although certain works of this period, for example *Restaurant*, are traditionally considered characteristic examples of Russian Cubo-Futurism. *Restaurant* is also unquestionably indebted to Italian Futurism with its clearly delineated fan-shaped composition tending towards the volumetric, spatial structure of Cubism and its introduction of fragments of text intended to evoke associations with and sensations of life in a big city, with its noise, increased rhythm and rapidly changing impressions. [E.B.]

131 Model, 1914 (p.64)
Oil on canvas. 106 × 71 cm
Inscribed by the artist on the back of the canvas: *Натурщица* [Model]; label of the Fine Arts Department; label of the Museum Fund with *No. 348*; label of the Museum of Artistic Culture
ЖБ-1712

132 Restaurant, 1915 (p.65)
Oil on canvas. 134 × 116 cm
On the back of the canvas: label of the Museum Fund with *No. 350*; label of the Museum of Artistic Culture
ЖБ-1334

Icons and Folk Art
By Irina Boguslavskaya

One of the artistic sources for the Russian avant-garde was folk art. The artists were genuinely impressed by its various forms: Kandinsky greatly admired the paintings on wood, Malevich was interested in textiles and embroidery, while Larionov collected *lubki* (popular prints) produced by different countries and peoples. There is evidence that the Museum of Artistic Culture also collected works of folk art, but the collection has not survived and its fate is unknown.

The works of folk art represented in the exhibition were mostly assembled from scientific expeditions of the State Russian Museum from 1960 to 1980. However, they give a very complete impression of the most typical objects in everyday use in the various Russian regions.

One remarkable piece of tableware for feast days was the *kovsh-skopar* [ladle], which served both as a table decoration and as a vessel for beer, kvass and home-brew. The kovsh is hollowed out of a whole stump and painted with large flowers. On the side is the inscription: 'This is the kovshyk of Lavrenty Ermolaev Polyakov Painted in 1868'. Inscriptions such as these are quite rare in folk art.

The painted sleighs of Northern Russia also served as ritual objects for young people during winter excursions.

The role of the distaff had great significance in peasant life: as a tool for spinning thread, a decoration for young girls' gatherings on winter evenings, and as a farewell wedding present from father to daughter before her departure to a new married life. In each region, therefore, distaffs had a particular form and construction and were differently decorated with carving, painting and a variety of colours. In the northern regions distaffs are particularly beautifully proportioned and are decorated with delicate geometric carving. In the Volga region it is the seat on which the spinner sits that is decorated. Once she had finished her spinning, she would hang the seat on the wall of the hut like a picture.

In the nineteenth century, with the proliferation of hotels and inns, trays started to come into great demand, both for utilitarian purposes and for interior decoration. In St Petersburg and the Moscow region workshops appeared where trays were painted with still lives and elegant bunches of flowers.

A particular area of folk art is occupied by toys. One of the most celebrated regions for wooden toys was Sergiev Posad near Moscow. Here they carved various miniature figures from blocks of wood: ladies, wet-nurses, nannies with children. These figures from different social levels were endowed with remarkable plasticity and decoration.

The artists of the Russian avant-garde derived inspiration from folk art, studying the purely formal techniques which could enrich their own creations.

133 Icon: The Almighty Saviour, Northern School, late 17th century
Tempera on wood. 89·5 × 75·4 cm
ДРЖ-2974

134 Icon: The Miracle of the Archangel Michael with Floros and Lavros, Northern School, late 17th century
Tempera on wood. 53·5 × 44 cm
ДРЖ-3041

135 Lubok: Mice Burying a Cat, 18th century
Facsimile reproduction of 18th-century engraving (photolithograph), coloured by hand
41·2 × 73·2 cm; image: 34·5 × 58·8 cm
Гр.луб.3378

136 Lubok: Song, 1884
Unknown artist (after the lithograph by Vasiliev)
Painted lithograph on paper. 34·8 × 45·3 cm; image: 22·7 × 34·7 cm
Гр.луб.1478

137 Lubok: The Heavenly Bird Alkonos (undated)
Unknown artist
Indian ink, pen and watercolour on paper. 48.8 × 40 cm; image: 39·6 × 31·5 cm
Дуб.2415

138 Ladle (Kovsh-Skopar), 1868
Made in Vetluzhsky, Kostroma province
Carved and painted wood. 24 × 68 × 41 cm
Inscribed on the side: *Сей ковшыкъ Лаврентия Ермолаева Полякова Крашен въ 1868 году* [This is the kovshyk of Lavrenty Ermolaev Polyakov Painted in 1868]
Р-3849

139 Sleigh, 1915
Solvychegodsk, Vologda province
Craftsman Andrei Zhitkov
Carved and painted wood. 74 × 29 × 36 cm
Р-2226

140 Distaff, late 19th century
Made in the region of Totemsky, Vologda province
Craftsman V.A. Tretyakov
Carved and painted wood. 87 × 22 × 40 cm
Д-2734

141 Distaff, 1873
Made in the region of Archangel, Archangel province
Carved and painted wood. 19 × 14 × 55 cm
Д-1999

142–144 Three Distaffs, second half of the
19th century
Made in the region of Gorodets, Nizhny Novgorod
province
Carved and painted wood. 62 × 8·5 × 19 cm
P-1412, 1413, 1414

145 Tray, 19th century
St Petersburg
Oil paint on metal. 56 × 71 × 4 cm
P-1547

146 Tray, 19th century
Moscow province, Godin Workshop
Oil paint on metal.
P-1556

147–151 Toys, 19th century
Sergiev Posad, Moscow province
Lady: 17·8 × 5·5 × 2·2 cm. Д-38
Wet-Nurse: 23·5 × 6·5 × 2 cm. Д-2320
Lady: 17 × 6·5 × 3·2 cm. Д-66
Nanny: 18 × 5 × 3 cm. Д-375
Doll: 17·2 × 5·9 × 1·6 cm. Д-2682

133

134

140

141

142

143

144

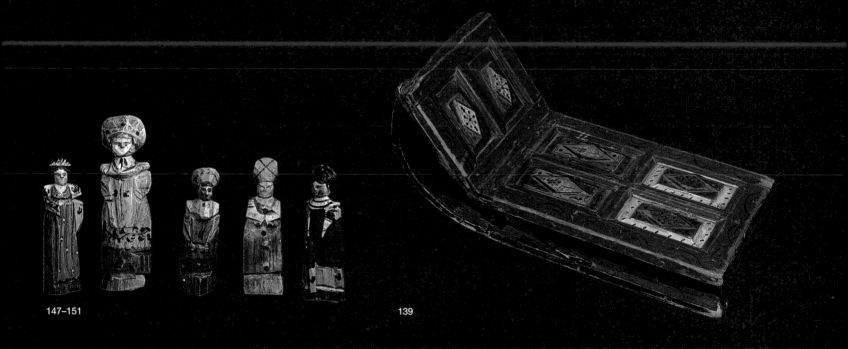

147–151

139

Kazimir Malevich and the Museum of Artistic Culture: Suprematist Porcelain

By Elena Ivanova

The Suprematists were attracted to porcelain, seeing in their industrially manufactured, everyday use an opportunity to put one of their theoretical postulates into practice – the move from easel painting to creating objects ('the making of things'). The 'half-cup' created by Malevich in turn exemplified the idea of economy in art: a rounded volume, cut in half, was both decreased by half and deprived of its familiar symmetry. The dissonance of contradictions – the rounded sides and flat vertical walls – achieved an effect of 'dynamic tranquillity'.

For Malevich's group, work on ceramic objects signified the move from two-dimensional Suprematism to volume. Nikolai Suetin composed his inkpot from geometric figures: beams, a cube, a segment (the base), and a large disc. The piece is presented like a model of Suprematist architecture in miniature. Its function is unclear; it is no accident that the first example of the ink-well had a lid that could not be removed.

Suetin's white vases also resemble architectural models. In proportion, plasticity and line, the white vessels are very close to the architectonic and construction moduli of the town of the Future, which the Suprematists dreamt of and planned.

The Suprematists were also attracted by the colour in porcelain. For them white was the definition of creative freedom. Sparkling whiteness and a subtly lit fragment were considerably more powerful than the bright surface of a canvas, and more capable of expressing the sensation of infinite cosmic space in which coloured geometrical constructions move about. The most striking example of this is Suetin's painting on the large plate with blue sides and the cup with an orange disk. Even when he had to paint on traditional porcelain objects, Suetin effortlessly achieved the impression of planes of colour in motion. The Suprematists worked most intensively with porcelain in 1923. Of all Malevich's pupils and followers, only Suetin remained faithful to the medium until the end of his life.

152 K.S. Malevich and I.G. Chashnik
Cup: Suprematism, 1923
Porcelain, painted underglaze. 12·5 × 6 × 7·2 cm
Mark of Unovis (Affirmers of New Art) on the back: framed black square; black hammer and sickle mark
СФ-27

153 K.S. Malevich and N.M. Suetin
Cup and Saucer: Suprematism, 1928
Porcelain, painted underglaze. Cup: 6·1 × 11 × 5·3 cm; *diam.* of saucer: 14·3 cm
СФ-517 а,б

154 N.M. Suetin
Dish: Suprematism, 1923
Porcelain, painted underglaze. *Diam.* 31·5 cm
СФ-9

155 N.M. Suetin
Ink-Well with Lid: Suprematism, 1923–4
Porcelain. 12·7 × 16 × 14·1 cm
СФ-29 а,б

156 N.M. Suetin
Cup and Saucer: Orange Disk, 1920s
Porcelain, painted underglaze. Cup: 7·5 × 11·7 × 9·3 cm; *diam.* of saucer: 15·8 cm
СФ-25 а,б

157 N.M. Suetin
Tea Service: Suprematism, 1930
Porcelain, painted underglaze. Teapot with lid (СФ-2157 а,б): 19 × 15·1 x 11·1 cm; milk jug with lid (СФ-2158 а,б): 13·5 × 10·3 × 8·3 cm; suger bowl with lid (СФ-2159 а,б): 10·2 × 13·2 × 10·6 cm; two cups and saucers (СФ-2160/1 а,б): 5·5 × 11·3 × 9·7 cm; *diam.* of saucer: 15 cm

158 N.M. Suetin
Plate: Suprematism, 1930
Porcelain, painted underglaze. *Diam.* 22·5 cm
СФ-10

159 N.M. Suetin
Oval Vase, 1930s
Porcelain. 22 × 12.7 × 7 cm
СФ-1338

160 N.M. Suetin
Architectonic Vase, 1930s
Porcelain. 23·5 × 12·5 × 12·5 cm
СФ-1336

161 N.M. Suetin
Four-Sided Vase, 1930s
Porcelain. 20 × 9·5 × 9·5 cm
СФ-1333

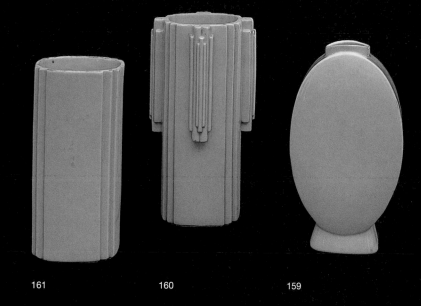

161 160 159

152 & 153

156

157

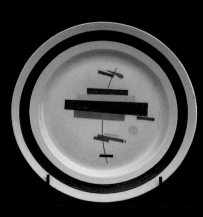

158 154

Russian Avant-Garde Posters
Irina Zolatinkina

Artists of the avant-garde first began working in the field of poster art in the years immediately following the Revolution. At that time poster art underwent a resurgence, becoming extremely topical in these years of great social upheaval. Although the avant-garde was not the only movement involved in creating a graphic language of poster art, the artists of the 'left' did play a significant role in the creation of a new type of poster, above all the political poster (which came to be recognised as an independent genre during the First World War). Creative innovation was combined with the innovative spirit of revolutionary ideas, and many of the avant-garde works are numbered among the best examples of poster art.

The three-dimensionality of the avant-garde's work was most clearly expressed in the posters for the Petrograd ROSTA. These Russian Telegraph Agency posters known as 'Okna ROSTA' [Russian Telegraph Agency Windows] were one of the most famous examples of agitation art in the first years of the revolution. An art department responsible for producing these 'okna' was set up in Moscow at the end of 1919 on the initiative of Vladimir Mayakovsky who headed the enterprise; similar departments soon appeared in other cities in the republic. The essence of the posters was graphically to convey 'telegraphic' political and economic news, revolutionary slogans and celebrations. Kozlinsky's poster *The Dead of the Paris Commune*, for example, was a response to a very popular theme of the time, drawing historical parallels with revolutionary events in France of the eighteenth and nineteenth centuries. The posters were run off by hand and quickly disseminated. The Moscow 'okna' were created using a stencil, while for the Petrograd ones they used linocuts which were then painted by hand.

In the spring of 1920 in Petrograd the 'Okna ROSTA' were organised by Vladimir Kozlinsky. He and Vladimir Lebedev were responsible for most of the posters produced at the time – more than a thousand over a two-year period. Kozlinsky and Lebedev developed a particular style of Petrograd poster that owed much in its general plastic construction to Cubism. Kozlinsky's

monumental works are more expressive and romantic; many are variations on the methods used by the artist for his series of linocuts entitled *St Petersburg 1919*. His poster entitled *Despite Three Years of Efforts by the Enemies of the Whole World, the Revolution is Making Giant Steps* is an undoubted creative success, with its word-for-word reproduction of the slogan and the red 'giant step' which became a striking symbol of the revolution's powerful force. Some of Lebedev's works were influenced by Suprematism: the poster *It is Necessary to Work – with a Rifle at your Side* represents a kind of ideal plastic formula created with Suprematist coloured planes.

The first half of the 1920s marked a new stage in the development of the advertising poster, the key figure being Alexander Rodchenko. His work is now regarded as the characteristic symbol of the era, with Constructivist aesthetics predominating in advertising. Rodchenko's work achieves its expressive quality through a laconic compositional combination of disconnected type, geometric Constructivist representation, colour saturation of individual planes, and the overall dynamic tension of graphic space. With Mayakovsky (who wrote the texts), Rodchenko created some 50 posters, more than 100 trade signs, covers, trade marks and advertising columns. One of the posters included here was a commission Rodchenko received from Mosselprom, designed to encourage the purchase of state beer. Another is from a series done in 1923-4 for the private *Dobrolet* (Volunteer Airforce) society which existed from 1923 to 1930.

162 V.I. Kozlinsky
Despite Three Years of Efforts by the Enemies of the Whole World, the Revolution is Making Giant Steps, 1920
Petrograd, ROSTA. Author of text: A.M. Flit
Colour linocut on two boards.
70.7 × 50 cm
Гр.пл.2319

163 V.I. Kozlinsky
The Dead of the Paris Commune have been Resurrected under the Red Banner of the Soviets, 1921
Petrograd, ROSTA
Painted linocut
72 × 47·7 cm
Гр.пл.1070

164 V.V. Lebedev
It is Necessary to Work – With a Rifle at Your Side, 1921
Petrograd, ROSTA. Author of text: V.V. Mayakovsky
Painted linocut
77·8 × 56·5 cm
Гр.пл.2324

165 A.M. Rodchenko
Buy Dobrolet Shares, 1923
Moscow
Chromolithograph
71·2 × 50·2 cm
Гр.пл.717

166 A.M. Rodchenko
Three Mountain Beer Will Drive Away the Hypocrite and
Home-brew, 1925
Moscow. Author of text: V.V. Mayakovsky.
Chromolithograph.
69·8 × 47·5 cm
Гр.пл.2125

162

163

Selected Bibliography
Publications in English

Bird, Alan, *A History of Russian Painting*, Phaidon, Oxford 1987

Bohm-Duchen, Monica, *Chagall*, Phaidon 1998

Bowlt, John (Ed), *Russian Art of the Avant-garde: theory and criticism 1902–1934* (revised edition), Thames and Hudson, London 1988

Dictionary of the Russian Avant-garde, Abrams, New York 1995

Cooke, Catherine, *Russian and Soviet Avant-garde, 1915–32: Art, Architecture and Design*, Guggenheim Museum Publications, New York 1992

Decter, Jacqueline, *Nicholas Roerich*, Thames and Hudson, London 1989

Decter, Jacqueline, *Nicholas Roerich: The Life and the Art of a Russian Master*, Parkstone Press 1992

Decter, Jacqueline, *Messenger of Beauty: Life and Visionary Art of Nicholas Roerich*, Parkstone Press 1997

Elliott, David, *'New Worlds': Russian Art and Society 1900–1937*, Thames and Hudson, London 1986

Gray, Camilla, *The Russian Experiment in Art 1863–1922* (revised edition), Thames and Hudson, London 1986

Hague Museum Palais Langue, Russian *Avant-garde, 1900–1930: Chudnovsky Collection from St Petersburg*, Snock-Ducaju and Zoon, Ghent 1995

Hahl-Koch, Jelena, *Kandinsky*, Thames and Hudson, London 1993

Kamenskii, Aleksandr, *Chagall: The Russian Years, 1907–22*, Thames and Hudson, London 1989

Kandinsky, Wassily (Lindsay, Kenneth and Vergo, Peter (Eds), *Kandinsky: Complete Writings on Art*, Da Capo Press, New York 1994

Kovtun, Evgeni, *Mikhail Larionov (1881–1964)*, Parkstone Press 1997

Kovtun, Evgeni, *Russian Avant-garde in the 1920s–1930s: Paintings, Graphics, Sculpture, Decorative Arts from the Russian Museum in St Petersburg*, Parkstone Press 1996

Leningrad, State Russian Museum; Tretiakov Gallery, Moscow, and the Stedelijk Museum, Amsterdam, *Kazimir Malevich 1878–1935* (exhibition catalogue), Stedelijk Museum, Amsterdam 1989

Margolin, Victor, *Struggle for Utopia: Rodchenko, Lissitzky, Moholy-Nagy, 1917–46*, University of Chicago Press, Chicago 1998

Messer, Thomas, *Kandinsky*, Thames and Hudson, London 1997

Milner, John, *Kasimir Malevich and the Art of Geometry*, Yale University Press, New Haven 1996

New York, Solomon R. Guggenheim Museum, *The Great Utopia: The Russian and Soviet Avant-garde 1915–1932* (exhibition catalogue), Guggenheim Museum Publications, New York 1992

New York, Museum of Modern Art, *Aleksandr Rodchenko* (exhibition catalogue), New York 1998

Noever, Peter (Ed), *Aleksandr M. Rodchenko and Varvara F. Stepanova: The Future is Our Only Goal*, Prestel Verlag, Munich 1991

Oxford, Museum of Modern Art, *Art into Production: Soviet Textiles, Fashion and Ceramics 1917–1935* (exhibition catalogue), Oxford 1984

Parsons, Thomas, *Malevich*, Studio Editions, London 1993

Parton, Anthony, *Mikhail Larionov and the Russian Avant-garde*, Thames and Hudson, London 1993

Poling, Clark, *Kandinsky – Russian and Bauhaus Years, 1915-33*, Guggenheim Museum Publications, New York 1983

Polonsky, Gill, *Chagall*, Phaidon, London 1998

Rodchenko, Aleksandr (Elliott, David and Lavrentiev, Alexander (Eds) *Alexander Rodchenko: Works on Paper, 1914–20*, Sotheby's Publications 1993

Rudenstine, Angelika, *Russian Avant-garde Art: The Costakis Collection*, Thames and Hudson, London 1981

Rudnitsky, Konstantin, *Russian and Soviet Theatre: Tradition and the Avant-garde*, Thames and Hudson, London 1988

Sarabyanov, Dimitri, *Russian Art: From Neoclassicism to the Avant-garde*, Thames and Hudson, London 1990

Stupples, Peter, *Pavel Kuznetsov: His Life and Art*, Cambridge University Press, Cambridge 1990

Vienna, Austrian Museum of Applied Arts in association with Mucsarnok, Budapest, *Art and Revolution, Russian and Soviet Art. 1910–1932* (exhibition catalogue), Locker Verlag, Vienna 1988

Washington, *Russian and Soviet Painting 1900–1930* (exhibition catalogue), Smithsonian Institute Press, Washington 1988

Weiss, Peg, *Kandinsky and Old Russia: The Artist as Ethnographer and Shaman*, Yale University Press, New Haven 1995

Wood, Paul, *Great Utopia: Russian and Soviet Avant-garde, 1915–1932*, Abrams, New York 1994

Index

Page references to illustrations are in italics